the
CREAMERY
kitchen

the CREAMERY kitchen

*Discover the age-old tradition
of making fresh butters, yogurts,
creams and soft cheeses at home*

Jenny Linford

photography by
Clare Winfield

RYLAND PETERS & SMALL
LONDON • NEW YORK

For Tash, who loved food and books

SENIOR DESIGNER Iona Hoyle

COMMISSIONING EDITOR Nathan Joyce

HEAD OF PRODUCTION Patricia Harrington

ART DIRECTOR Leslie Harrington

EDITORIAL DIRECTOR Julia Charles

PROP STYLIST Lisa Harrison

FOOD STYLIST Rosie Reynolds

INDEXER Hilary Bird

ILLUSTRATIONS Diana Newnham

First published in 2014 by
Ryland Peters & Small
20–21 Jockey's Fields, London
WC1R 4BW
and
Ryland Peters & Small Inc.
519 Broadway, 5th Floor
New York, NY10012

www.rylandpeters.com

10 9 8 7 6 5 4 3 2 1

Text © Jenny Linford 2014
except recipes listed on the right
Design and photographs
© Ryland Peters & Small 2014
except page 12 © Benjamin Hole

ISBN: 978-1-84975-494-1

A CIP record for this book is available
from the British Library.

US Library of Congress cataloguing-in-
publication data has been applied for.

Printed and bound in China

NOTE

• All eggs are medium (UK) or large (US)
unless otherwise specified

RECIPE CREDITS

All recipes © Jenny Linford with the
following exceptions:

page 38 Chloe Coker and Jane
Montgomery; page 41 Maxine Clark;
pages 42 and 84 Hannah Miles;
pages 90 and 93 Isidora Popovic;
pages 111 and 112 Julian Day; page 118
Ross Dobson; page 121 Tonia George

contents

introduction

Dairy foods, such as butter, cream and yogurt, have a special place in our affections. Although these are normal ingredients which we use every day – spreading butter on toast, drinking a refreshing glass of milk, enjoying a lunchtime yogurt – they are also treats, with a pleasurably indulgent aura about them.

One of the particular qualities of dairy foods, which make them so enduringly popular, is their remarkable versatility as ingredients. Their characteristically delicate, simple flavour means that they can be used in both sweet and savoury dishes, as the varied recipes in this cookbook demonstrate. As well as their flavour, texture forms a huge part of their appeal – whether the light-textured, barely-set quality of natural yogurt, the seductive velvetiness of mascarpone or the smooth creaminess of butter. Traditionally, dairy products have been valued for the textures that they bring to dishes, whether the luxurious richness created by adding in double/heavy cream or butter, the elegant delicacy which ricotta has as an ingredient or the ethereal fluffiness of whipped cream. They can be used both as a finishing touch – melting a small piece of fragrant spice butter onto a freshly fried pancake – or simply as an accompaniment, with the tanginess of a dollop of crème fraîche, for example, nicely counterpointing a rich dessert, or as a main

ingredient in their own right, used to make
cheesecakes, dumplings or savoury dips. Given
that all dairy foods have one ingredient – milk –
as their starting point, the range of textures
and subtly varying flavours within them is
remarkable – a testimony to both milk's
extraordinary properties as a foodstuff and
human beings' culinary ingenuity.

This book shows you how simple it is to make your
own dairy products at home. Processes such as
transforming cream into butter or milk into yogurt –
both gloriously easy – are wonderful acts of kitchen magic,
carrying with them a glow of satisfaction. Having made your
own cream cheese or crème fraîche, for example, this book also
offers an appetizing collection of recipe ideas of how to cook
with these wonderful foods, inspired by cuisines around the
world, from French to Middle Eastern. Once your interest is
aroused, you will find yourself looking at milk, cream and yogurt
in a new light – as the starting points from which to make other,
lovely dairy products such as labneh or buttermilk. Have fun
exploring the wonderful world of the home creamery.

creating your creamery

While making your own dairy products at home is simple, there is one golden rule that is vital to observe – the importance of good hygiene. Visit any dairy operation or cheesemaker and it is clear that cleanliness is paramount and the same requirement also applies to a domestic situation. Be absolutely scrupulous in making sure that all the equipment you use is meticulously clean, sterilizing kit where necessary. The surface area where you're working should be clean and tidy. Before you start, have everything you will require to hand. The need for cleanliness, of course, also applies when it comes to washing your own hands. It's important to be aware of the risks of cross-contamination, with frequent hand-washing recommended to maintain a sanitary environment. Making dairy products often involves a period where the ingredients are left to stand. In these cases, do use a protective covering to keep insects off and to ensure that nothing falls into the ingredients.

In terms of the equipment needed to make dairy products, most of them are everyday kitchen items, so it is very simple to get started. There are a few key items though which you will need:

· An accurate, detailed kitchen thermometer, ideally with an easy-to-read dial so that you can monitor the subtle changes in temperature that cheesemaking requires. Sugar thermometers feature higher temperatures than used in cheesemaking and often lack the detailed temperature information that you'll need. Thermometers, which can be clamped to the side of the pan, allowing you to monitor the changes in temperature as you work, are a good idea.

· A large, heavy-based pan, in which to heat the milk

· Large, fine-meshed muslin/cheesecloth squares (for straining)

· String, for tying up the muslin/cheesecloth

· Large metal spoons (slotted and un-slotted), for transferring curd

· A long-bladed knife to cut the curds

· A food processor (to make the butter)

· Cheese moulds/molds (not essential, only if you wish to shape the cheeses)

· Coeur à la crème moulds/molds (for making the heart-shaped coeurs à la crème)

basic ingredients

Milk, of course, is the starting point for all dairy products. Although usually the word 'milk' is taken to imply cow's milk, there are other animals whose milk humans use for drinking and for making dairy products from, notably sheep, goats and water buffalo. Milk from these four species has differing characteristics and flavour:

Cow's milk has a creamy colour and is rich in fat, which is naturally present in large fat globules.

Sheep's milk, noticeably white in colour, is high in fat and protein, with its small fat molecules evenly distributed throughout the milk, making it easily digestible.

Goat's milk is bright-white in colour and has a high fat content. The fat is present in small particles, and therefore easy for the stomach to process.

Water buffalo's milk is brilliant-white in colour and is high in calcium, protein and lactose. Like sheep's milk, its small fat particles are evenly distributed throughout the milk, making it similarly easy to digest.

As well as milk, many dairy products require the addition of 'starter cultures' and also rennet, both of which affect the flavour and texture of the milk. 'Starter cultures' or 'starters', consist of specific bacteria that transform the milk by consuming lactose (milk sugar) and producing lactic acid, creating both a subtle sour tang and thickening the milk. Cultured buttermilk and 'live' yogurt can be used as starter cultures. It is also possible to buy specialist starter cultures, which can be used to make specific dairy products, such as mascarpone or crème fraîche. Acidifiers – such as lemon juice or vinegar – are also used to begin this souring, thickening process.

Rennet is a substance obtained from the stomach lining of mammals (usually cows) containing the enzyme rennin, which is used to coagulate milk. Historically, small, dried pieces of rennet were added to the milk to begin the process of coagulation, during which solid masses (curds) separate from the liquid (whey).

It is possible to buy animal rennet in liquid or powder form. Vegetarian rennets – made from bacterial sources, fungal sources or genetically modified mico-organisms – are also available.

buying milk & cheese

By the time we buy milk, this most natural of foods has usually been pasteurized (a process that heats milk, usually to 71.7°C (161°F) for 15 seconds, so killing all bacteria) and homogenized (a process that breaks down the natural butterfat found in the milk and distributes it throughout the milk). Longlife or UHT (ultra-heat treatment) milk has been heated to very high temperatures to extend its shelf-life, a process which affects its flavour, giving it a 'cooked' taste.

Furthermore, milk is available with differing fat contents: skimmed/fat-free (with a fat content of 0–0.5%), semi-skimmed/low-fat (with a fat content of 1.7%), whole milk (with a minimum fat content of 3.5%) and natural whole milk, with no fat removed or added.

Organic milk is produced in accordance to organic regulations and comes from cows grazed on pasture that has not been treated with chemical fertilizers, pesticides or agrichemicals. In the UK and in several US states, unpasteurized and unhomogenised milk, also known as 'raw' milk, can be bought direct from the dairy farmers producing it, either at the farm itself or at farmers' markets. This milk will taste subtly different at different times of year, according to what the cows are fed. For example, milk produced in spring or summer, when the cows are usually grazing on lush pastures, may have a subtle sweetness, which differs from their winter milk, when they are fed silage. Another point of difference arises from the breed of cows in the dairy herd. The milk from Jersey and Guernsey cows, for example, is noted for its high butterfat content and rich yellow colour. While goat's milk is increasingly available, sheep's milk and buffalo's milk (from water buffalo) are much harder to find on supermarket shelves, although the internet makes finding sources much easier.

Cream is the part of milk that is high in butterfat. In unhomogenized milk, the cream rises naturally to the surface. However, modern commercial milk production involves using centrifugal force to separate the cream from the milk. As with milk, cream is sold with different fat contents: single/light cream (less than 18% in the UK, but 18–30% fat in the US), double/heavy cream (no less than 48% fat in the UK, but no less than 36% in the US) and whipping cream (no less than 35% fat in the UK, but 30–36% fat in the US). Goat's cream, white in colour and with a distinctive, slightly nutty flavour, can be found, though it is not widely available.

When it comes to keeping milk and cream, they are both perishable, so should be stored in the refrigerator. If shopping for them at farmers' markets or buying direct from a dairy farm, do make sure to take a chilled bag to keep them cool while you're out.

BUTTER

Butter, ranging in colour from the palest of primrose yellows to deep golden yellow and with its distinctive smooth texture, has a special place in our culinary affections.

Despite butter's wide availability, it continues to be considered a little bit of a treat, an indulgence. The phrase 'all-butter' carries a cachet, a promise that quality ingredients have been used with results that you will notice in terms of taste. In Western cuisine, butter is a hugely important ingredient, used to add flavour and texture to everything from pastry to roux-based sauces.

Historically, transforming cream into butter was a way of extending the life of precious but perishable cream. Butter is made by churning cream until the butterfat within the cream comes together. The butter is then salted or not, as desired, with the salt acting both as a flavouring and a preservative. Traditionally it was made by hand, using a butter-churn, with the butter then patted into shapes or moulded, using specially carved moulds. Today, most butter is industrially produced from cream that has been extracted using centrifugal force, using butter-making machinery. Although the vast majority of butter is made from cow's cream, it can also be made from the cream of goats, sheep and water buffalo.

We tend to think of 'butter' as if it was simply one food, but there are actually various types of butter. 'Sweet cream' butter, which is made from fresh cream, is generally characterized by a mild, creamy flavour. 'Cultured cream butter', also known as 'lactic butter', is made from cream to which lactic acid bacteria has been added, allowing the cream to 'ripen' and take on a slight tang, with the resulting butter similarly flavourful. This style of butter is associated with continental Europe, with highly-prized French butters, such as Échiré, a fine example of this style. 'Whey butter' is a distinctively sweet butter made from cream separated from whey during the cheese-making process.

If you like butter, it's well worth experimenting and sampling different butters. Good cheesemongers, delicatessens and farmers' markets are often a fruitful source of craft butters. As with many foods, there is a notable difference between a carefully-made, artisan butter and the mass-produced version. As butter taints very easily, absorbing other flavours, the freshness of the butter you buy is another factor which will affect its flavour.
Making it yourself, of course, allows you to enjoy it very fresh!

MAKING BUTTER

If you have a food processor, then making your own butter is gloriously simple. One of the joys of making it is that you are able to eat truly fresh butter; you will be able to taste the difference. Experiment with cream from different producers. Goat's butter, bright white and with a distinctive, slightly nutty flavour, can be made by simply substituting goat's double/heavy cream for cow's cream in the recipe to the right.

ingredients

300 ml/1¼ cups whipping cream or double/heavy cream, at room temperature

500 ml/2 cups very cold water

salt, to taste

equipment

food processor

sieve/strainer

potato masher

ramekins

waxed paper

butter pats (optional)

makes about 130 g/ 9 tablespoons

Place the cream in a food processor and blend for a few minutes until it separates into pale yellow butter and a milky-white liquid, the latter of which is the buttermilk. Transfer the contents of the food processor to a sieve/ strainer to drain off the buttermilk, which can be drunk or used for cooking.

You now need to remove the buttermilk remaining in the butter, as otherwise it will turn rancid and spoil the butter. Return the butter to the food processor and add in 100 ml/a scant ½ cup of very cold water. Blend briefly, then drain off the cloudy liquid. Repeat the process four more times until the liquid running off is practically clear.

Place the butter in a large bowl and work it with a potato masher to bring the butter together and to press out any remaining moisture. Drain off any liquid as it comes out.

Season the butter with salt to taste and continue mashing until it is smooth, firm and so that no more liquid escapes from it.

Transfer the butter to a ramekin or mould/mold or simply shape using a spoon or butter pats. Wrap in waxed paper and store in the fridge.

FLAVOURED BUTTERS

fennel butter

A sophisticated flavoured butter, particularly good with fish such as salmon or sea bass.

1 teaspoon fennel seeds

50 g/3½ tablespoons butter, softened

2 tablespoons finely chopped fennel fronds

¼ teaspoon Pernod or Ouzo (optional)

makes 50 g/3½ tablespoons

Dry-fry the fennel seeds in a small, heavy-based frying pan/skillet until fragrant, around 1–2 minutes. Cool and finely grind.

Using a fork, mix together the butter, ground fennel seeds, fennel fronds and Pernod or Ouzo, if desired. Cover and chill or freeze until required.

caramelized butter

Use this rich butter to add flavour and richness to soups and stews.

40 g/3 tablespoons butter

makes 40 g/3 tablespoons

Place the butter in a small saucepan. Gently heat until the butter melts and white sediment appears. Continue cooking over a very low heat, stirring now and then, until the white sediment turns brown and the butter has a nutty fragrance. Remove from the heat and use at once.

piquant butter

This butter is fantastic for barbecues – try it on griddled sweetcorn or beef steaks.

50 g/3½ tablespoons butter, softened

2 teaspoons chilli/hot red pepper flakes

½ teaspoon paprika

makes 50 g/3½ tablespoons

Using a fork, mix together the butter, chilli/hot red pepper flakes and paprika until thoroughly incorporated. Cover and chill or freeze until required.

fragrant spice butter

Great as a breakfast treat, try this sweet butter on hot toast, crumpets or pancakes.

50 g/3½ tablespoons unsalted butter, softened

2 tablespoons light brown soft sugar

1 teaspoon ground cinnamon

½ teaspoon freshly grated nutmeg

½ teaspoon ground ginger

makes 50 g/3½ tablespoons

Using a fork, mix together the softened butter, sugar and spices until well-mixed. Cover and chill or freeze until required.

rose butter

Delicately fragrant, this is lovely on freshly-baked scones, crêpes or toast.

50 g/3½ tablespoons butter, softened

½ teaspoon rose water

2 tablespoons icing/confectioners' sugar

3 teaspoons crystallized rose petals, finely crushed

makes 50 g/3½ tablespoons

Using a fork, mix together the butter, rose water, sugar and crushed crystallized rose petals until well mixed. Cover and chill or freeze until required.

saffron butter

Use this glorious orange-yellow butter on grilled white fish or roast chicken.

3 generous pinches of saffron strands

50 g/3½ tablespoons butter, softened

makes 50 g/3½ tablespoons

Finely grind the saffron strands using a pestle and mortar. Mix with ½ teaspoon hot water and set aside to infuse for 15 minutes. Using a fork, mash the cooled saffron water into the softened butter, incorporating well. Cover and chill or freeze until required.

SPANISH SPICED POTTED SHRIMPS

Potted shrimps in spiced butter is a traditional British dish. Using Spanish paprika adds colour and a distinctive smoky flavour. Serve as a starter with warm bread or toast.

180 g/12 tablespoons butter

finely grated zest of 1 unwaxed lemon

pinch of salt

1 teaspoon sweet smoked Spanish paprika

½ teaspoon hot smoked Spanish paprika

freshly ground black pepper

200 g/6½ oz. peeled shrimps

toasted bread, to serve

4 ramekins

serves 4

Gently melt the butter in a small saucepan over a low heat. Once melted, stir in the lemon zest, the salt, sweet paprika, hot paprika and freshly ground black pepper.

Add the peeled shrimps to the spiced butter in the saucepan and mix well.

Divide the shrimps and spiced butter mixture evenly between the ramekins. Allow to cool, cover and chill until serving. Serve with toasted bread.

LIME SHORTBREAD WEDGES

These rustic-looking, crumbly-textured biscuits/cookies go well with cream-based desserts, and can also be enjoyed simply with a cup of tea or coffee.

175 g/12 tablespoons unsalted butter, softened

80 g/⅓ cup plus 1 tablespoon caster/granulated sugar

finely grated zest of 2 unwaxed limes

170 g/1⅓ cups plain/all-purpose flour

75 g/⅔ cup rice flour or ground rice

20-cm/8-in. cake pan, loose-based and well-oiled

makes 12

Preheat the oven to 170°C (325°F) Gas 3.

In a mixing bowl, cream together the butter and sugar until well mixed. Mix in the lime zest.

Place a sieve/strainer over the mixing bowl containing the butter and sugar and sift the flour and rice flour. Quickly mix the flours, butter and sugar together to make a soft, crumbly dough.

Place the dough on a lightly-floured work surface and knead briefly to bring together.

Press the soft dough into the prepared cake pan to an even thickness. Using the back of a knife, mark the dough circle into 12 even-sized triangular sections. Prick the shortbread dough lightly with a fork.

Bake the dough in the preheated oven for 45 minutes until golden-brown. Allow to cool in the pan for 10 minutes, before transferring onto a rack. While still warm, cut the shortbread into the triangular wedges.

These shortbread wedges will keep in an airtight container for 1 week.

BUTTERMILK

Traditionally buttermilk, as its name suggests, was a by-product of butter-making. It was made from the white, milky liquid created when cream was transformed into butter, which was then allowed to further 'ripen', during which time it would thicken and sour slightly.

Nowadays, the buttermilk available to domestic consumers has usually been created by adding cultures to milk and allowing it to ferment. Characteristically, buttermilk is white in colour with a subtly thick texture, reminiscent of yogurt, and with a faintly sour tang in flavour. Traditionally, it has long been regarded as a healthy drink, appreciated for its low fat content, and, in the case of buttermilk containing 'live' probiotics, thought to be beneficial for digestion.

As with other dairy foods, buttermilk can be used for numerous culinary reasons. It's excellent in baking and is particularly valued for the way in which it creates a tender crumb and light texture, for example, in Irish soda bread, American cornbread and scones. It's a useful ingredient when it comes to breakfast dishes, whether fruity buttermilk smoothies (used in place of yogurt to add a subtle sour note) or fluffy American-style pancakes. In Scandinavian cuisine, in which tangy dairy products such as drinking yogurt are much enjoyed, buttermilk is used in dishes such as Denmark's sweet 'buttermilk soup',

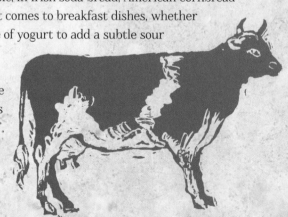

which is served cold as a dessert during spring and summer. Its distinctive flavour makes it an excellent ingredient to use in desserts, such as the Panna Cotta with Cloudberry Coulis (page 32). Alternatively, use it as a refreshing base ingredient for home-made ice cream to create both a pleasant richness and a refined touch of acidity.

Buttermilk's natural acidity also makes it a useful ingredient in marinades for meat or poultry, as it has a tenderizing effect. Buttermilk Fried Chicken (page 28), in which the chicken is marinated with buttermilk, spices and other flavourings before being deep-fried to crisp, golden-brown glory, is probably the best-known example of this. This subtle tang also makes it a good ingredient for salad dressings, used to cut the richness of mayonnaise, for example, or added to a vinaigrette for extra texture and flavour. Its refreshing qualities mean that a swirl of buttermilk, added to say a deep purple-coloured, cold beet(root) soup or a rich, orange butternut squash one, adds both a striking visual note and a pleasant flavour contrast.

MAKING BUTTERMILK

This useful dairy ingredient, with its delicately thick texture and faint sour tang, can be made very simply at home by triggering a 'ripening' process in milk, which causes the milk to thicken and take on a subtle sharpness. All that's needed in order to start this process is either lemon juice or white wine vinegar. Please note that in the US, buttermilk is only so-called if a culture has been added to it; otherwise, it is known as 'sour milk'.

ingredients

500 ml/2 cups whole milk, at room temperature

2 tablespoons white wine vinegar or freshly squeezed lemon juice

equipment

sterilized glass jar

muslin/cheesecloth

30-cm/12-in. length of string

makes 500 ml/2 cups

Place the room-temperature milk in a large mixing bowl. Add the vinegar or lemon juice and mix them well.

Set the mixture aside for 15 minutes, during which time the milk will thicken slightly and take on a faintly sour tang.

Store the buttermilk in a sterilized jar covered with muslin/cheesecloth tied up with string, in the refrigerator. It will keep for up to 1 week.

BUTTERMILK FRIED CHICKEN

Making a marinade with buttermilk to coat drumsticks
before frying them makes for tender, flavourful chicken.
This is a thoroughly tasty dish, and very much a family
favourite. Serve with crunchy coleslaw on the side.

2 garlic cloves, crushed

1 thumb-sized piece of root
ginger, crushed

½ teaspoon chilli powder

1 teaspoon chopped fresh
thyme leaves

300 ml/1¼ cups buttermilk

salt and freshly ground
black pepper

8 chicken drumsticks

200 g/1½ cups plain/
all-purpose flour

1 teaspoon ground ginger

sunflower oil, for
deep-frying

serves 4

In a large bowl, mix together the garlic, ginger, chilli,
thyme and buttermilk to make the marinade. Season
well with salt and freshly ground black pepper.

Add the chicken drumsticks to the marinade bowl and
coat them well. Cover and chill in the fridge for 8 hours
or overnight.

In a separate bowl, mix together the flour and ground
ginger and season with salt and pepper. Transfer this flour
mixture to a large plate.

Shake any excess marinade from the chicken drumsticks
and coat them thoroughly in the seasoned flour.

Pour the oil into a large, deep frying pan/skillet to around
2 cm/¾ in. depth and allow the pan to become very hot.
Test the the pan is the right heat by dropping in a small
piece of bread; if it turns brown very quickly, the oil is
hot enough.

Add in the chicken drumsticks (cooking them in batches
if the pan isn't large enough for them all) and fry until
they are a rich golden-brown on all sides, around 15–20
minutes. Remove the chicken drumsticks from the pan,
allow them to rest on paper towels or another absorbent
surface to soak up the oil and serve immediately.

PARMESAN BUTTERMILK SCONES

Buttermilk makes for wonderfully light scones. Here, Parmesan cheese is used to give a subtle, rich cheesy flavour to savoury scones.

250 g/2 cups self-raising/
self-rising flour

a pinch of salt

1 teaspoon baking powder

50 g/3 tablespoons butter,
diced

50 g/²⁄₃ cup finely grated
Parmesan cheese, plus extra
for topping

1 egg

125 ml/¹⁄₂ cup buttermilk,
plus extra for glazing

*6-cm/2¹⁄2-in. diameter
cookie cutter*

baking sheet, greased

makes 8

Preheat the oven to 220°C (425°F) Gas 7.

Sift the flour, salt and baking powder into a large mixing bowl. Next, rub in the butter with your fingertips until it is absorbed into the mixture. Stir in the grated Parmesan and mix well.

In a separate bowl, use a fork to lightly whisk together the egg and buttermilk. Now add it to the flour mixture and lightly fold it in to form a soft, sticky dough.

Roll the dough out on a lightly floured work surface to 2.5 cm/1 in. thickness and use the cookie cutter to cut out 8 scones.

Place the scones on the prepared baking sheet. Brush each scone with a little buttermilk and sprinkle with a little grated Parmesan.

Bake in the preheated oven for 10–15 minutes until they have risen and are golden-brown.

These are particularly good eaten warm from the oven, sliced in half with a little butter.

BUTTERMILK PANNA COTTA
with cloudberry coulis

Using buttermilk in panna cotta gives it a lovely, subtle flavour.
The ivory-coloured panna cotta together with the orange
cloudberry or mango makes a very pretty, elegant dessert.

8 g/approx. 4 sheets leaf
gelatine

300 ml/ 1¼ cups
double/heavy cream

75 g/⅓ cup vanilla sugar or
caster/granulated sugar

300 ml/1¼ cups buttermilk

1 teaspoon vanilla bean paste

for the coulis

6 tablespoons cloudberry
jam (if cloudberry jam is
hard to find, use 200 ml/
6½ oz. canned Alphonso
mango pulp instead)

1 tablespoon freshly
squeezed orange juice

*6 ramekins or similar
small serving bowls*

makes 6

Soak the leaf gelatine in cold water for 5 minutes,
then squeeze dry.

In a small pan, gently heat together the double/heavy
cream and sugar, stirring until the sugar has dissolved.
If using caster/granulated sugar rather than vanilla
sugar, add a little more vanilla bean paste later when
stirring in the buttermilk.

Remove from direct heat, add in the soaked gelatine
and stir in well, until the gelatine has dissolved.

Transfer to a bowl and stir in the buttermilk and
vanilla paste, mixing together well.

Divide the buttermilk mixture among 6 ramekins or
small serving bowls. Cool, cover and chill until it has
set, around 3 hours.

To serve, mix together the cloudberry jam and orange
juice. Spoon a little of the cloudberry coulis over the
top of each panna cotta and serve. Alternatively, dip
the bowls briefly in hot water, carefully turn out the
panna cottas onto serving plates and spoon over
the cloudberry coulis and serve.

SOUR CREAM

Although the term 'sour cream' might imply a culinary mishap, the sourness is intentional. It is made from single/light cream that has been deliberately soured by adding a specific bacterial culture. The bacteria consume the lactose (milk sugar) in the cream and create lactic acid which thickens and sours the cream, giving it a refreshing tartness.

Sour cream is an ingredient particularly associated with the cuisines of Central and Eastern Europe, classically added in a last minute element to cut through the richness of dishes such as Hungary's flavourful goulash or, an East European classic, borscht. Mexico's crema (a similar product to sour cream but with a lighter texture) is similarly used to contrast with spiced dishes. A classic use for it, inspired by its East European heritage, is served alongside smoked salmon or caviar and dainty blinis (yeast pancakes), with the refreshing tartness of the bright, white sour cream offering an excellent foil to the salty fattiness of the smoked salmon or caviar and the buckwheat-flavoured intensity of the blinis. In its role as tangy 'garnish', it's widely eaten as a topping with baked potatoes, classically topped with finely chopped chives and fresh flat-leaf parsley.

One thing to be aware of when using it in cooking is that sour cream, when heated, can easily curdle, creating a granular texture. This is why many recipes for cooked dishes featuring sour cream will caution removing the dish 'from the heat' and only then stirring in the sour cream. Also, despite being a member of the cream family, it can't be whipped.

Its versatility, though, means that it can be used in many ways. The fact that it can be eaten without cooking makes it a simple-to-use base for numerous tasty dips, flavoured with everything from finely chopped fresh herbs to cooked beans or blue cheese. Similarly, it is a useful base for salad dressings, combined, for example, with sliced cucumber and mixed with finely chopped, aniseed-flavoured dill. Its use, however, is not just restricted to savoury dishes: sour cream, with its delicate richness, can also be used to good effect in numerous sweet dishes, including Sour Cream Raisin Pie (page 41). Flavoured with vanilla extract, a layer of sour cream poured onto baked cheesecake and then baked for a short time to set, offers an appealing extra dimension both in terms of flavour and texture.

MAKING SOUR CREAM

A versatile dairy ingredient, sour or soured cream is very simple indeed to make at home. Do take note, however, that several hours are required for the process of 'souring' to take place. Fortunately, however, the cream can simply be set aside during this time. Single/light cream rather than rich double/heavy cream is the starting point, giving sour cream its characteristic texture. Cultured buttermilk is added and mixed in, triggering a slow process whereby the single/light cream thickens and takes on the subtle sourness that the name 'sour' cream implies.

ingredients

300 ml/1¼ cups single/light cream

3 tablespoons cultured buttermilk

equipment

muslin/cheesecloth

30-cm/12-in. length of string

makes about 350 ml/1½ cups

In a large bowl, mix together the single/light cream and buttermilk.

Cover the bowl with muslin/ cheesecloth tied with string and set aside at room temperature for 7–10 hours until thickened. Chill until required.

CHILLED CUCUMBER & MINT SOUP
with Parmesan crisps

This refreshing chilled soup is perfect for a warm summer's day. If you aren't a fan of chilled soups, give this recipe a try and be converted. It's easy to make in advance and will keep for a day in the fridge, ready to serve. The Parmesan crisps add extra texture but are optional.

6 cucumbers, peeled, cored, and chopped into chunks

a small handful of fresh mint, roughly chopped

480 ml/2 cups sour cream or crème fraîche

freshly grated zest of 1 unwaxed lemon and freshly squeezed lemon juice, to taste

1½ garlic cloves, crushed

1 teaspoon sugar

salt and freshly ground black pepper

for the Parmesan crisps (optional)

50 g/1¾ oz. Parmesan cheese, finely grated

baking sheet lined with parchment paper

serves 4–6

Preheat the oven to 180°C (350°F) Gas 4.

Put the cucumbers and mint in a food processor and blitz to a purée. Push the purée through a fine mesh sieve/strainer using the back of a ladle — it will look quite watery.

Put half of the pulp left in the sieve/strainer back into the blender along with the watery mixture. Add the crème fraîche/sour cream, lemon zest, garlic, sugar and salt and pepper, then blend until combined. Taste the mixture and season with lemon juice, sugar and salt and pepper. This soup needs to be highly seasoned to bring out the delicate flavours.

To make the crisps, spread thin strips of Parmesan onto the prepared baking sheet. Ensure you leave a good space between each strip as they will spread in the oven.

Bake the crisps in the oven for 7 minutes until the Parmesan melts and colours slightly. Take them out of the oven and gently remove the crisps from the baking sheet using a palette knife. Put the crisps on a rack until cooled and crisp.

Ladle the soup into serving bowls and put an ice cube in each bowl of soup to keep it well chilled. Top with the Parmesan crisps and serve immediately.

SOUR CREAM RAISIN PIE

This is almost like a very light cheesecake baked in a double crust – very rich and luscious. Serve it with extra whole raisins plumped up in sweetened rum overnight. This is always best served cold as it will be too soft to cut if warm.

for the pie crust

375 g/3 cups plain/
all-purpose flour

a good pinch of salt

250 g/1 cup plus 2
tablespoons white cooking
fat/shortening, chilled and
diced

1 egg, beaten

1 tablespoon white wine
vinegar

4 tablespoons ice-cold water

for the pie filling

150 g/1 cup large juicy
raisins, chopped

3 tablespoons spiced rum

2 large eggs

225 g/1 cup plus 2
tablespoons caster/
granulated sugar

250 ml/1 cup sour cream

1 tablespoon freshly
squeezed lemon juice

¼ teaspoon freshly grated
nutmeg

2–3 tablespoons demerara/
raw brown sugar, for
dredging

23-cm/9-in. metal pie plate
baking sheet lined with
parchment paper

serves 4–6

Preheat the oven to 230°C (450°F) Gas 8 and set a heavy baking sheet on the middle shelf. Soak the chopped raisins in the rum for an hour until the rum is absorbed.

Sift the flour and salt into a large mixing bowl and cut in the fat with two round-bladed knives until thoroughly combined. (You can also do this in a food processor.) In a separate bowl, mix together the beaten egg, vinegar and water. Pour this wet mixture into the dry mixture and cut it in with the knives again.

Tip out onto a lightly floured surface and knead lightly until smooth, then shape into a flattened ball. Wrap in clingfilm/plastic wrap and chill for at least 30 minutes.

Divide the pastry dough into 2 pieces. Roll one half out on a lightly floured surface and use it to line the pie plate. Trim off the excess pastry.

Use an electric hand whisk to whisk the eggs with the caster/granulated sugar until the mixture is pale and mousse-like. Set aside.

Reserve 2 tablespoons of the sour cream for the glaze. Whip the remaining sour cream with the lemon juice, nutmeg and salt until slightly thickened. Carefully fold into the egg mixture, then fold in the soaked chopped raisins. Spoon into the pie crust.

Roll out the remaining pastry thinly so that it will cover the top of the pie. Brush the edges of the pie with a little water, pick up the pastry on the rolling pin and lift it over the pie to cover it. Fold the top crust carefully under the lower crust and press the edges together to seal.

Brush with the reserved sour cream and dredge with the demerara/raw brown sugar. Slash the top a couple of times to allow the steam to escape. Place the pie on the baking sheet in the preheated oven and bake for 10 minutes. Reduce the oven temperature to 180°C (350°F) Gas 4 and bake for a further 20 minutes until the crust is set and pale coloured. Leave to cool before serving.

SWEETCORN MUFFINS

These lovely gluten-free muffins are an ideal
accompaniment to soup. Packed with both puréed corn
and whole kernels, they're moist and full of flavour.

200 g/1²⁄₃ cups gluten-free
self-raising/self-rising flour
plus 1 teaspoon baking
powder

OR 1²⁄₃ cups gluten-free
plain/all-purpose flour plus
2³⁄₄ teaspoons baking
powder and 1¼ teaspoons
xanthan gum

1 teaspoon bicarbonate of
soda/baking soda

50 g/¹⁄₃ cup fine yellow
cornmeal (preferably stone-
ground)

330 g/1²⁄₃ cups
sweetcorn/corn kernels

150 ml/²⁄₃ cup milk

2 eggs

4 tablespoons sour cream
or crème fraîche

100 g/6½ tablespoons butter,
melted and cooled

1 tablespoon
caster/granulated sugar

salt and freshly ground
black pepper

*2 muffin pans lined with
16 muffin cases*

makes 16

Preheat the oven to 180°C (350°F) Gas 4.

Sift the flour, baking powder (plus xanthan gum, if using)
and bicarbonate of soda/baking soda into a mixing bowl
and stir in the cornmeal.

Blitz half of the sweetcorn/corn kernels to a smooth purée
in a food processor, then add it to the flour mixture.

In a separate bowl, whisk together the milk, eggs, sour
cream or crème fraîche and melted butter, then add to the
flour mixture. Whisk everything together well, adding the
sugar and seasoning with salt and pepper. Stir through
most of the remaining whole sweetcorn/corn kernels,
reserving a few kernels to sprinkle on top of the muffins.

Divide the mixture between the muffin cases and top
with the remaining corn. Bake in the preheated oven for
25–30 minutes until golden brown and the muffins spring
back to your touch. Serve warm or cold.

The muffins will keep for up to 2 days in an airtight
container but can be frozen and then reheated to serve.

CRÈME FRAÎCHE

As its name implies, this is traditionally a French dairy product. Although a literal translation would be 'fresh cream', in fact, crème fraîche is made commercially from double/heavy cream to which a specific lactic bacterial culture is added; this culture consumes the lactose (milk sugar) in the cream, so causing it to thicken noticeably and take on a perceptible sour flavour.

Normandy, in northern France, is particularly noted for its production of crème fraîche. The most famous French crème fraîche is produced by Normandy-based dairy co-operative, Isigny Sainte Mère; in 1986, it was granted a prestigious 'Appellation d'origine contrôllée (AOC)' regulating and protecting the way in which it makes its crème fraîche. At Isigny Sainte Mère, bacterial culture is added to locally-produced cream, which is then left to ripen at room temperature for 18 hours. This slow maturation process results in a distinctive velvety-textured, thick, tangy crème fraîche.

Its high fat and low protein content, means that crème fraîche can be cooked without curdling, making it a very versatile dairy product. It is used to give a sour rich note to a wide range of dishes from chicken korma to the brunch classic omelette Arnold Bennett. Within French cuisine, this distinctive dairy product has many uses, whether it is added to soups, braised dishes, salad dressings, tossed with vegetables or used in fillings for savoury flans, such as crab tart, where it can be substituted for double/heavy cream. Many of France's classic sauces – such as bonne femme – are enriched with crème fraîche, Normandy, as one might expect given its history of production, is especially rich in traditional dishes which use it, such as Sole Normande, an intricate fish dish featuring a gloriously indulgent crème fraîche sauce, and the dish Faisan à la Normande, pheasant with a Calvados (another traditional Normandy product) and crème fraîche sauce.

Crème fraîche's culinary uses, however, are not restricted to savoury dishes. It is also much used in French pâtisserie and confectionery, in everything from cherry tart to salted caramels. With its seductive texture and sophisticated tang, one of the easiest ways of using crème fraîche is simply as an accompaniment to desserts, especially rich ones such as dark chocolate mousse cake or wine-poached, spiced pears.

MAKING CRÈME FRAÎCHE

With its subtle sour tang, crème fraîche is a sophisticated ingredient, used to add richness to dishes such as savoury flans, braised dishes and sauces. Despite its luxurious reputation, crème fraîche is very simple indeed to make at home – all it needs is time! The starting point for crème fraîche is smooth-textured, butterfat-rich double/heavy cream. Then, cultured buttermilk is added, which triggers the process by which the cream thickens and takes on a slight sharpness.

ingredients
300 ml/1½ cups double/heavy cream
3 tablespoons cultured buttermilk

In a mixing bowl, mix together the double/heavy cream and buttermilk.

Cover and set aside at room temperature for 7–10 hours until the mixture has thickened. Chill until required.

makes about 350 ml/1½ cups

FLAVOURED CRÈME FRAÎCHE

herbed crème fraîche salad dressing

Using crème fraîche in salad dressings gives a rich and creamy texture and a slight, pleasing sourness.

90 ml/6 tablespoons crème fraîche

1 tablespoon olive oil

1 tablespoon white wine vinegar

1 teaspoon Dijon mustard

1 tablespoon chopped chives

2 tablespoons finely chopped fresh flat-leaf parsley

1 tablespoon finely chopped fresh tarragon leaves

salt and freshly ground black pepper

makes about 120 ml/½ cup

Use a fork to whisk together the crème fraîche, olive oil, vinegar and mustard until they're well-mixed. Stir in the chives, parsley and tarragon. Season with salt and pepper and serve.

roast chilli crème fraîche

There's something very appealing about this combination of velvety-textured crème fraîche and spicy chillies/chiles! Use one or more peppers according to taste. Serve it with barbecued meats or poultry for a fiery kick!

1–3 large red chilli/chile peppers

200 ml/1 scant cup crème fraîche

salt and freshly ground black pepper

1 tablespoon chopped fresh coriander/cilantro

makes about 200 ml/ 1 scant cup

Preheat a grill/broiler. Place the chilli/chile peppers on an oven rack and grill/broil until charred on all sides, a matter of minutes.

Wrap the charred chillies/chiles in a plastic bag and set aside to cool. Once cooled, peel and carefully, de-seed them, then chop them into small pieces.

Fold together the chillies/chiles and crème fraîche and season with salt and pepper. Chill until serving.

Sprinkle with coriander/cilantro just before serving.

salted caramel crème fraîche sauce

An indulgent sweet treat, serve this sauce with good vanilla ice cream, baked bananas or pancakes.

75 g/$\frac{1}{3}$ cup caster/granulated sugar

100 ml/scant $\frac{1}{2}$ cup water

50 g/3$\frac{1}{2}$ tablespoons unsalted butter

100 ml/scant $\frac{1}{2}$ cup crème fraîche

1 teaspoon sea salt flakes

makes about 180 ml/¾ cup

Place the caster/granulated sugar and water in a small, heavy-based saucepan. Cook over a medium heat, stirring, until the sugar has dissolved.

Increase the heat, bring to a bubbling boil and cook without stirring until the syrup thickens and turns dark gold in colour.

Reduce the heat and carefully stir in the butter. Stir in the crème fraîche, mixing it in thoroughly and then mix the salt until it has dissolved.

Serve this sauce warm or at room temperature.

red berry crème fraîche

A simple but stylish accompaniment to desserts, particularly good with chocolate mousse cake!

170 g/generous 1 cup raspberries, thawed if frozen

300 ml/1$\frac{1}{4}$ cups crème fraîche

1 tablespoon icing/confectioners' sugar

a few drops of vanilla extract

makes about 400 ml/1¾ cups

Blitz the raspberries into a purée in a food processor or blender. Pass the raspberry purée through a fine mesh sieve/strainer to remove the seeds.

Mix together the crème fraîche, sugar and vanilla extract. Lightly swirl the purée into the crème fraîche, creating a marbled effect. Chill until serving.

BEETROOT LATKES
with smoked salmon
& crème fraîche

Serve this strikingly colourful dish as a first course or for brunch. Cool, silky crème fraîche contrasts well with salty smoked salmon and the slightly sweet, earthy-tasting, crisp-textured beet(root) latkes.

150 g/5 oz. raw beet(root)

150 g/5 oz. potatoes, peeled

½ red onion, peeled

1 egg, beaten

50 g/½ cup medium matzo meal

salt and freshly ground black pepper

sunflower oil, for frying

200 g/6½ oz. smoked salmon

4 dollops of crème fraîche

finely chopped fresh chives, to garnish

baking sheet lined with parchment paper

serves 4

Peel the beet(root) and trim off the trailing root. Hold each beet(root) by the stalk end and grate them coarsely. Grate the potato and the red onion.

In a large bowl, mix together the grated beet(root), potato and onion. Add in the egg, matzo meal, salt and pepper to taste and mix together thoroughly to form a thick, sticky mixture.

Preheat the oven to 160°C (325°F) Gas 2.

Pour the oil to a depth of 0.5 cm/¼ in. into a heavy-bottomed frying pan/skillet and heat it up thoroughly.

Fry the latkes in batches. Add 4 separate spoonfuls of the mixture, spaced well apart, to the hot oil, pressing each down lightly with the spoon to spread it out. Fry them for 3 minutes, then flip each one over and fry for a further 2 minutes. Carefully remove the fried latkes from the pan and onto the prepared baking sheet before placing them in the oven to keep warm.

Repeat the process four times, making 12 latkes in all.

Serve the beet(root) latkes with smoked salmon and a dollop of crème fraîche topped with chopped chives.

ORANGE SYRUP SEMOLINA CAKE
with crème fraîche

This soft, moist, buttery cake contrasts nicely with the tangy crème fraîche on the side and makes an excellent dessert, with a small espresso coffee on the side.

for the cake

150 g/10 tablespoons butter, softened

175 g/³⁄₄ cup plus 2 tablespoons caster/granulated sugar

grated zest and freshly squeezed juice of ¹⁄₂ orange

2 eggs

100 ml/6 tablespoons crème fraîche

125 g/1 cup plain/all-purpose flour, sifted

1 teaspoon baking powder

125 g/1 cup plus 2 tablespoons fine semolina

a pinch of salt

for the orange syrup

juice of 1 large orange

150 g/³⁄₄ cup caster/granulated sugar

1 teaspoon orange flower water

crème fraîche, to serve

loose-based 20 cm/8 in. cake pan

serves 8

Preheat the oven to 180°C (350°F) Gas 4.

In a mixing bowl, cream together the butter and sugar until well-mixed. Add the orange zest and juice, then the eggs, one at a time, followed by the crème fraîche and mix well. Add the flour, baking power, semolina and salt and fold in. Transfer to the cake pan and bake in the preheated oven for 1 hour until golden-brown.

While the cake is baking, prepare the orange syrup. Place the orange juice and sugar in a small saucepan and gently heat, stirring, until the sugar has dissolved. Turn off the heat and wait until the pan has cooled, then mix in the orange flower water.

Test whether or not the cake is ready by piercing with a fine skewer; if it comes out clean, the cake is cooked, if not, bake it for a few minutes longer.

Remove the cake from the oven and place it on a rimmed baking sheet. While warm, pierce the top of the cake all over with a skewer. Pour over the orange syrup, then cover the cake and set it aside to cool and soak up the syrup, a few hours or overnight.

Serve in slices with crème fraîche on the side.

YOGURT

Made by fermenting milk, yogurt is an ancient foodstuff, made for thousands of years in Central and Western Asia and India. Its distinctive sharp, sour flavour is created by adding specific bacteria that consume the lactose (milk sugar), releasing lactic acid and thickening the milk. Unlike indulgent cream or crème fraîche, yogurt has long had an aura of 'healthiness' about it, valued in particular for its digestive qualities.

Nowadays, yogurt is available in many forms including different fat contents, ranging from fat-free to full-fat. 'Natural' yogurt is free from any added flavourings, with a light texture and refreshing sour flavour. In the UK, 'Greek' yogurt is the term given to yogurt that has been strained, resulting in a thicker texture and a milder flavour. 'Live yogurt' denotes the presence of living, benign bacteria in the yogurt; whereas long-life or UHT yogurt (which has been heat-treated to extend its life) does not contain these living bacteria. 'Bio' yogurt contains specific bacteria that are regarded as good for the digestive system, such as Bifidobacteria and Lactobacillus acidophilus.

Within these general categories, flavours and textures will range subtly but noticeably depending on the different producers, so it's worth sampling the options to find your favourites. Then there is the use of different milks to make yogurt from, with goat's milk yogurt and sheep's milk yogurt each having their own distinctive flavour.

Yogurt, with its mild flavour and light texture, lends itself to both sweetening and flavouring, as witnessed by the huge range of commercially made yogurts, flavoured with everything from strawberry to toffee. Natural, unflavoured yogurt, however, remains the most flexible, making an excellent accompaniment to fruit compotes or cereal, eaten simply with a little honey stirred into it, and often used to enrich fruit smoothies. In fact, there is a long tradition in countries with a venerable history of making and consuming yogurt of using yogurt diluted with cold water to make refreshing drinks, such as sweet or salty lassi in India or ayran in Turkey. Its pleasant sourness comes into its own in dips, such as Greek tzatziki (in which yogurt is mixed with cucumber, garlic and mint) or Indian, Pakistani and Bangladeshi raita, often served as a side-dish to contrast pleasantly with richly spiced curries.

Yogurt's acidity means that it is a useful base marinade ingredient, and works well tenderizing meat and poultry. When it comes to cooking with yogurt, however, do bear in mind that it needs stabilization, either by adding in cornflour/cornstarch or egg yolks, to prevent it from curdling.

Making your own yogurt is a very simple and rewarding process. Making it yourself, again, offers the chance for experimentation with different milks and in creating different textures.

MAKING YOGURT

This recipe uses full-fat cow's milk, but you can use other milks such as lower-fat cow's milk, goat's milk or sheep's milk. In order to trigger the fermentation process, 'live' yogurt needs to be added, which will be labelled as such on the pot. The yogurt should be incubated in a warm place, such as an insulated cooler box, in which you can place a couple of sealed jars of freshly boiled water in order to raise the temperature.

ingredients

800 ml/3¼ cups whole milk

3 tablespoons 'live' yogurt

equipment

kitchen thermometer

*large sterilized jar or a couple of
small sterilized jars*

makes 600 ml/2½ cups

Place the milk in a heavy-based saucepan. Heat the milk gently until it reaches 85°C (185°F), checking the temperature with the thermometer. Remove from the heat and allow it to cool for 10–15 minutes until the temperature lowers to 43°C (110°F). Now mix the 'live' yogurt into the warm milk.

Carefully pour the mixture into the sterilized jar or jars. Cover and set aside to incubate in a warm place (see opposite) for 7–8 hours until set to your taste.

The yogurt will keep in a refrigerator for up to 1 week.

yogurt 57

SPINACH YOGURT SOUP
with caramelized butter

Using yogurt in this delicately-flavoured soup gives it a subtle tang. For a light meal, serve it with crusty bread.

2 tablespoons olive oil

1 onion, finely chopped

1 teaspoon ground cumin

½ teaspoon chilli/hot red pepper flakes

800 ml/3¼ cups chicken or vegetable stock

salt and freshly ground black pepper

1 bunch of spinach, chopped

225 g/scant 1 cup yogurt

1 egg

2 teaspoons plain/all-purpose flour

40 g/3 tablespoons butter

a sprinkling of ground sumac (optional)

serves 4

Heat the olive oil in a large, heavy-based frying pan/skillet. Add the onion and fry gently, stirring often, for 5 minutes, until softened. Sprinkle in the cumin and chilli/hot red pepper flakes and mix together.

Add the stock, season with salt and pepper and bring to the boil, then reduce the heat and simmer gently for 5 minutes.

Meanwhile, caramelize the butter by gently melting it in a small saucepan until a white sediment appears. Continue cooking over a very low heat, stirring now and then, until the white sediment turns brown and the butter has a nutty fragrance.

While the butter is caramelizing, add the spinach to the simmering soup and cook gently for 2–3 minutes.

Meanwhile, whisk together the yogurt, egg and flour until well-mixed. Add the yogurt mixture to the gently simmering soup and continue cooking over a low heat for 3–4 minutes. Stir continuously and make sure that the soup does not come to the boil.

Stir in the caramelized butter, sprinkle with sumac, if desired, and serve at once.

ROASTED RED PEPPER, POMEGRANATE & SUMAC RAITA

Serve this colourful, cooling side-dish as an accompaniment to spicy curries or grilled meats.

2 red (bell) peppers

1 teaspoon balsamic vinegar

1 teaspoon olive oil

pinch of salt

400 g/1⅔ cups Greek yogurt

seeds of ½ a pomegranate

1 teaspoon sumac

serves 4–6

Grill/broil or roast the red (bell) peppers until they're charred on all sides. Wrap in a plastic bag (which makes them easier to peel afterwards), set aside to cool, then peel, de-seed and chop into short strips. Put the red (bell) pepper strips in a bowl, add the balsamic vinegar, olive oil and salt and mix together.

Fold the red (bell) pepper strips into the yogurt and stir in most of the pomegranate seeds, but set aside 1 tablespoon to garnish. Now stir in ½ teaspoon sumac.

Just before serving, garnish the raita with the reserved pomegranate seeds and sprinkle the remaining sumac over the top.

YOGURT GELATO

Based on traditional whole yogurt, this dessert is much creamier and more indulgent than when it's made with its fat-free relation. It's perfect served with a berry sorbet; alternatively, top with honey and toasted almonds or simply with fresh fruit.

500 ml/2 cups whole milk

50 ml/scant ¼ cup whipping cream

1 vanilla bean, split lengthways

160 g/¾ cup plus 1 tablespoon caster/granulated sugar

1 egg white

250 g/1 cup yogurt

fresh raspberries, to serve (optional)

ice cream or gelato maker

serves 4

Put the milk and whipping cream in a small saucepan and heat gently until it reaches boiling point. Pour the mixture into a heat-resistant bowl, add the vanilla bean and stir. Refrigerate for 20 minutes.

In a large mixing bowl and using an electric hand whisk, beat together the sugar and egg white until it forms soft peaks when the beaters are lifted out of the mixture. Stir in the yogurt.

Remove the chilled milk mixture from the refrigerator and discard the vanilla bean. Pour the milk mixture into the sugar and egg mixture and whisk for a further 20 seconds.

Pour the mixture into the ice cream maker and churn according to the manufacturer's instructions.

The gelato is best served immediately or can be kept in the freezer for up to 3–4 days.

LABNEH

This historic Middle Eastern foodstuff is also known as 'yogurt cheese' and is made from yogurt, wrapped in muslin/cheesecloth and suspended to remove moisture, resulting in a smooth-textured, tangy-tasting cheese with a texture similar to cream cheese.

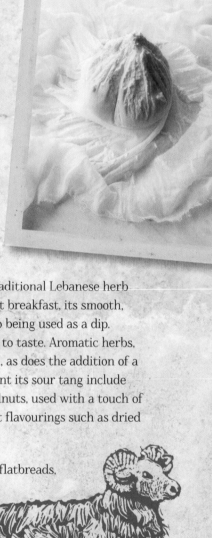

In Lebanon, labneh is traditionally a breakfast dish, served with flatbreads such as manakeesh bil za'atar, an olive oil-rich flatbread flavoured with a pungent, traditional Lebanese herb mixture. When it comes to eating labneh other than at breakfast, its smooth, spreadable texture means that it readily lends itself to being used as a dip. Its subtle flavour means that it can easily be seasoned to taste. Aromatic herbs, such as basil, rosemary, chervil, or thyme all work well, as does the addition of a little crushed garlic. Other ingredients that complement its sour tang include pitted olives, nuts, especially walnuts, pistachios, hazelnuts, used with a touch of argan oil or walnut oil for extra nuttiness, and piquant flavourings such as dried chilli/chile flakes or smoked Spanish pimentón.

Traditionally, labneh-based dips would be served with flatbreads, but do experiment with crispbreads, oatcakes, slices of good quality sourdough or soda bread. Fresh vegetable crudités, of course, also go well with labneh dips, from crunchy crimson radishes to sliced green (bell) pepper. In the Middle East, one traditional use for labneh is to shape it into small balls, set these aside to dry for several hours, then store them in olive oil, so allowing the labneh to be preserved for months.

The fact that labneh is so simple to make at home, allows the home cook to experiment with different types of yogurt – low-fat and full-fat, sheep's milk, goat's milk – and taste for yourself the subtle variations in texture and flavour that result. If you make your own yogurt to start with, then the possibilities of exploring the world of milk – using, say rich Jersey milk to make yogurt that you then transform into labneh – really begin to open up.

MAKING LABNEH

Labneh is a Middle Eastern dairy creation. Sometimes called 'yogurt cheese' it is made very simply by straining yogurt through muslin/cheesecloth overnight. The result is a smooth-textured 'cheese' with a fresh, slightly tangy flavour. Using sheep's or goat's milk yogurt produces labneh that is bright white in colour, with a more pronounced sour tang than labneh made using cow's milk yogurt.

ingredients
500 g/2 cups Greek yogurt

¼ teaspoon salt (optional)

equipment
muslin/cheesecloth

30-cm/12-in. length of string

long wooden spoon

Line a large bowl with a square of clean muslin/cheesecloth

Mix the yogurt and salt (if using) together well. Place the yogurt in the centre of the muslin/cheesecloth square. Wrap the muslin/cheesecloth up around the yogurt and tie it firmly with a long piece of string.

Suspend the muslin/cheesecloth parcel over a deep, large mixing bowl by tying it with the string to a wooden spoon laid across the top of the bowl.

Leave in the fridge for 24 hours. Then, unwrap and use as required.

makes about 350 g/1½ cups

labneh 67

LAMB SKEWERS
with za'atar labneh

Labneh, flavoured here with za'atar, a Middle Eastern herb mix, makes an excellent, tangy accompaniment to marinated lamb. Weather permitting, this would be a great dish for the barbecue. Serve it simply with Dukkah Flatbreads (page 72) and a side salad for a taste of summer.

for the skewers

2 tablespoons olive oil

freshly squeezed juice of 1 lemon

2 garlic cloves, crushed

1/4 teaspoon dried oregano

salt and freshly ground black pepper

600 g/1¼ lbs. lamb neck fillet, cut into even-sized cubes with sides around 2.5 cm/1 in.

8 cherry tomatoes

1 red (bell) pepper, chopped into even-sized squares with sides around 2.5 cm/1 in.

1 red onion, chopped into even-sized squares with sides around 2.5 cm/1 in.

for the za'atar labneh

350 g/1½ cups labneh

1 tablespoon za'atar

1 tablespoon olive oil, plus extra for serving

1 tablespoon pistachio nut kernels, finely chopped

serves 4

First, marinate the lamb for the skewers. In a large bowl, mix together the olive oil, lemon juice, garlic and oregano and season well with salt and pepper. Add in the lamb cubes and mix until they're well coated with the marinade. Cover with clingfilm/plastic wrap and marinate in the fridge for 1–8 hours.

Take the lamb out of the fridge and bring it to room temperature before cooking. Preheat the grill/broiler to its highest setting. Thread the lamb onto skewers, alternating the meat with cherry tomatoes and sliced red pepper and onion squares. Reserve the marinade remaining in the bowl.

Place the lamb skewers on an oven tray/broiler pan and grill/broil until cooked through, around 15 minutes, turning them over halfway through cooking. Brush the meat now and then with the reserved marinade so that it stays moist.

Meanwhile, make the za'atar labneh by mixing together the labneh, za'atar and olive oil. Place the labneh in a serving bowl. Using the back of a spoon, make a shallow hollow in the centre of the labneh. Pour in a little olive oil and sprinkle over the chopped pistachios.

Serve the freshly grilled lamb skewers with the za'atar labneh on the side.

ASPARAGUS, PEA & LABNEH SALAD

The taste of summer on a plate, this simple, vibrant salad can be served as an elegant first course or as an accompaniment to cold meats.

300 g/10 oz. asparagus spears, trimmed

½ tablespoon olive oil

salt and freshly ground black pepper

200 g/¾ cup fresh peas or 80 g/¾ cup frozen peas, thawed

350 g/1½ cups goat's milk or sheep's milk labneh

25 g/3 tablespoons flaked almonds

2 teaspoons lemon zest

a few fresh sprigs of flat-leaf parsley, to garnish

ridged grill pan

serves 4

Preheat a ridged stovetop grill pan. Toss the asparagus spears with the olive oil and season with salt and pepper. Dry-fry the asparagus for 2–3 minutes on each side, until lightly charred. Set aside and allow to cool.

Add the flaked almonds to the ridged stovetop grill pan and dry-fry until they're golden brown. Set aside and allow to cool.

Blanch the peas in boiling water for 2 minutes. Then drain, refresh in cold water to stop the cooking process and drain again.

Assemble the salad, by placing the fried asparagus and blanched peas in a serving dish. Top with spoonfuls of labneh, then sprinkle over the flaked almonds and lemon zest. Garnish with parsley leaves and serve at once.

DUKKAH FLATBREADS
with herbed labneh

Dukkah, a Middle Eastern nut and spice mixture traditionally used as a dip, gives a delicious flavour and texture to these flatbreads, which contrasts nicely with the tangy labneh.

500 g/3¼ cups strong white bread flour

1 teaspoon instant yeast

1 teaspoon sugar

1 teaspoon salt

300 ml/1¼ cups hand-hot water

2 tablespoons olive oil

for the dukkah

40 g/⅓ cup shelled hazelnuts

40 g/½ cup sesame seeds

1 tablespoon ground coriander

1 tablespoon ground cumin

½ teaspoon dried chilli/hot red pepper flakes

salt and freshly ground black pepper

for the herbed labneh

350 g/1½ cups sheep's milk or cow's milk labneh

1 small garlic clove, crushed

3 tablespoons finely chopped fresh flat-leaf parsley

2 tablespoons finely chopped fresh chives

1 teaspoon finely chopped fresh thyme leaves

serves 4

In a large bowl mix together the flour, yeast, sugar and salt. Add in the hand-hot water and olive oil and mix together to form a sticky dough. Transfer to a lightly floured work surface and knead for 5 minutes until elastic and smooth. Cover the dough with a tea/dish towel and rest in a warm place for 1 hour until it has risen.

Meanwhile, dry-fry the hazelnuts and sesame seeds in a small, heavy frying pan/skillet over a medium heat, stirring often, for 3–4 minutes until they begin to take on a golden-brown colour; set them aside to cool, transfer to a food processor and blend briefly until they're finely chopped. Mix in the coriander, cumin and chilli/hot red pepper flakes and season with salt and pepper.

Make the herbed labneh by gently folding in the garlic and chopped herbs. Cover and chill until required.

Knock back (punch down the dough and then gently knead briefly) the dough and place on a floured work surface. Sprinkle 4 tablespoons (store the rest in an airtight container) of dukkah into the centre of the dough, fold the dough over and knead it well for a few minutes.

Divide the flatbread dough into 8 even-sized portions and roll out each portion into a thin oval shape. Preheat a large, heavy frying pan/skillet until hot. Cooking them in batches, place the flatbread onto the frying pan/skillet and cook over a high heat for around 2 minutes until the flatbread begins to puff and bubbles form on the surface. Using tongs, turn over the flatbread and cook for a further 1–2 minutes, before transferring them to an oven on a low heat to keep warm. Repeat the process until all the flatbreads have been cooked.

Serve the warm dukkah flatbreads at once with the herbed labneh.

SAFFRON & CARDAMOM LABNEH with mango

This rich and fragrant dairy-based dessert is an exotic, pleasantly indulgent way in which to round off a meal.

2 pinches of saffron strands

2 green cardamom pods

350 g/1½ cups cow's milk labneh

3 tablespoons icing/confectioners' sugar, sifted

2 medium mangoes, peeled and sliced

1 tablespoon finely ground pistachio kernels

serves 4

Finely grind the saffron. Mix with 1 teaspoon of freshly boiled water and set aside to infuse for 15 minutes.

Crack the green cardamom pods and remove and finely grind the black seeds with a pestle and mortar, discarding the husks.

Fold together the labneh, icing/confectioners' sugar, cooled saffron water and ground cardamom, mixing in well. Cover with clingfilm/plastic wrap and chill.

To serve, divide the mangoes among 4 serving bowls. Top with saffron labneh, sprinkle with the ground pistachio kernels and serve.

CREAM CHEESE

With its mild flavour, soft, spreadable texture and versatility, cream cheese is enormously popular. It is made from milk enriched with cream, with the latter giving the cheese its gentle richness of flavour and texture.

Cream cheese's delicate, neutral taste means that it can be readily flavoured. It is often combined with garlic and finely chopped herbs, such as chives or parsley, to create a tasty dip or mixed with crabmeat, grated Cheddar and flavourings to make Maryland crab dip. Its soft texture lends itself as a filling, for example, in chicken breast fillets, which are then coated and fried, with the cream cheese creating a soft, moist filling. Flavoured with ingredients such as chopped spring onion/scallion, diced chorizo or feta cheese and dill, cream cheese is also a popular filling for mushrooms or piquant jalapeño peppers or, rolled inside filo/phyllo pastry, for tasty, deep-fried nibbles such as variations on Turkish burek. Cream cheese's spreadable nature also makes it a very popular cheese for easily assembled snacks, whether sweet creations such as cream cheese and banana sandwiches – or as a vehicle for savoury ingredients, such as that classic Jewish delicacy smoked salmon and cream cheese bagels.

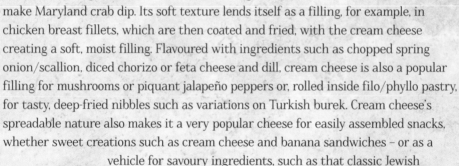

Its subtle creamy flavour means that cream cheese can equally be used in many desserts, with sweetened cream cheese, flavoured with vanilla and mixed with eggs, a standard ingredient in baked cheesecakes. American baking features several ingenious uses of cream cheese, in sweet treats such as muffins or cream cheese pound cakes. It also works well dotted into cake mixtures to provide a contrast in flavour and texture, such as cream cheese chocolate brownies. Cream cheese is ideal to use as frosting – simply beat together cream cheese with sifted icing/confectioners' sugar and a little lemon juice until well-mixed. For extra richness, mix in a little softened butter, using food colourings to colour as you please. A classic cream cheese frosting is an integral part of carrot cake's appeal – try adding orange juice and grated zest for an extra citrus kick.

MAKING CREAM CHEESE

Making a soft cheese, such as cream cheese, is the simplest way in which to begin exploring the joys of cheesemaking. This recipe involves enriching whole milk both with cream, which gives the cheese a gentle richness of flavour and texture, and 'live' yogurt. It is then heated and later curdled by adding rennet, before being set into curds, cut and drained. This transformation of simple ingredients into a soft cheese is enormously satisfying to make. The freshly made cream cheese will keep in the refrigerator for up to 2 weeks.

ingredients

600 ml/2½ cups whole milk

400 ml/1⅔ cups double/heavy cream

100 ml/scant ½ cup 'live' yogurt

5 drops of cheese-making rennet, dissolved in a little boiled and cooled water

salt

equipment

kitchen thermometer

shallow, slotted spoon

muslin/cheesecloth

colander

30-cm/12-in. length of string

makes 200–300 g/1–1⅓ cups, depending on draining time

Mix together the milk, cream and yogurt in a large, heavy-based saucepan. Gently heat the mixture to 100°F (38°C), checking it with a thermometer. Then, remove from the heat and stir in the rennet mixture and the salt. Stir for 2–3 minutes during which time the milk will begin to curdle. Cover the saucepan with a lid and set aside for 1 hour until the curd has set.

Using a shallow, slotted spoon, cut through the mixture right down to the bottom of the pan. Make this first 'cut' in the centre of the pan, then perform the same movement at roughly 2.5 cm/1 in. intervals to the left and right of the centre until you reach both edges of the pan. This will allow the curds to separate from the whey. Using the same spoon, carefully remove the curds from the pan, draining off the whey as you do so.

Place the curds in a muslin-/cheesecloth-lined colander standing on a deep plate. Gather the muslin/cheesecloth together and squeeze the curds to drain off excess whey. Tie the muslin/cheesecloth with string and suspend the parcel over the colander by attaching string to a long wooden spoon placed across the colander's rim. Leave for at least 8 hours to drain.

Remove the cream cheese from the muslin/cheesecloth, add a little salt and mix in well. Store chilled in the refrigerator for up to 2 weeks.

cream cheese 79

CREAM CHEESE & OLIVE PARCELS

These delicious, Mediterranean-flavoured nibbles are perfect appetizers to serve with drinks.

1 teaspoon olive oil

3 spring onions/scallions, finely chopped

200 g/1 cup cream cheese

40 g/⅓ cup pitted green olives, chopped

1 tablespoon finely chopped fresh dill

freshly ground black pepper

6 rectangular filo/phyllo sheets

50 g/3½ tablespoons unsalted butter, melted

sesame seeds, for garnish

baking sheet, greased

makes 12

Preheat the oven to 200°C (400°F) Gas 6.

Heat the olive oil in a small frying pan/skillet and fry the spring onions/scallions until softened. Set aside until cool.

In a mixing bowl, mix the cream cheese, fried spring onions/scallions, olives and dill. Season with a generous grinding of black pepper.

Slice the filo/phyllo sheets in half lengthways, forming 12 rectangular strips.

Brush one of the strips with melted butter (keeping the remaining sheets covered with clingfilm/plastic wrap to prevent them drying out). Place a generous teaspoon of the cream cheese mixture on the buttered filo/phyllo strip 2 cm/1 in. from the bottom. Take the bottom left corner of the strip and fold it up and over the filling, to form a triangular shape, then across again to the other side. Continue until you have formed a tightly closed triangular parcel. Brush on a little extra melted butter to seal the last flap into place and then place on a baking sheet. Brush the parcel generously with melted butter and sprinkle over a few sesame seeds.

Repeat the process with the remaining filo/phyllo strips, making 12 parcels in total.

Bake them in the preheated oven for 15–20 minutes until golden-brown. Serve warm or at room temperature.

COEUR À LA CRÈME
with strawberries & passion fruit

This classic French dish makes an elegant dessert, though do bear in mind that ideally you should start preparing it the day before you plan to serve it. Combining it with fresh fruit, such as strawberries and passion fruit or with apricot compote and raspberries, helps to offset the richness.

200 g/1 cup cream cheese

150 ml/²⁄₃ cups double/heavy cream

1 tablespoon vanilla sugar or caster/granulated sugar

½ teaspoon vanilla bean paste (optional)

4 ripe passion fruits, halved

200 g/1 pint strawberries, chopped into halves

4 heart-shaped coeur à la crème moulds/molds

4 muslin/cheesecloth squares

serves 4

Line 4 heart-shaped coeur à la crème moulds/molds with 4 muslin/cheesecloth squares.

In a large bowl, use a balloon whisk to gently whisk together the cream cheese, double/heavy cream, sugar and vanilla bean paste until thoroughly folded together.

Divide the cream cheese mixture evenly among the 4 lined moulds/molds. Gently fold the muslin/cheesecloth over the filling, covering it completely.

Place the moulds/molds in a baking pan or a deep dish and set aside for at least 8 hours in the refrigerator.

To serve, carefully remove each cream cheese heart from its mould/mold and onto serving plates. Spoon some passion fruit pulp around each heart and decorate each plate with strawberries.

WHISKY & RASPBERRY CRANACHAN CHEESECAKES

This cheesecake is inspired by the classic Scottish dessert, cranachan – whipped cream flavoured with whisky and honey folded through with toasted oats and fresh raspberries.

for the base

50 g/3½ tablespoons butter

30 g/2½ tablespoons caster/granulated sugar

40 g/2 tablespoons golden/light corn syrup or maple syrup

100 g/1 cup (old-fashioned) rolled oats

a pinch of salt

for the filling

150 g/1¼ cups raspberries

80 ml/⅓ cup whisky

300 g/1⅓ cups cream cheese

300 ml/1¼ cups crème fraîche or double/heavy cream

80 ml/¼ cup honey

2 eggs

generous 1 tablespoon plain/all-purpose flour, sifted

to serve

a handful of fresh raspberries

pouring cream

baking sheet, greased

8 x 6-cm/2½-in. diameter chef's rings, greased and placed on a greased baking sheet

makes 8

Preheat the oven to 170°C (325°F) Gas 3.

For the base, heat the butter, sugar and golden/corn or maple syrup together in a saucepan until the butter and sugar have melted and the mixture is syrupy. Stir in the oats and salt and mix well so that all the oats are coated.

Spoon the mixture onto the prepared baking sheet and flatten with the back of a spoon. Bake in the preheated oven for 20–30 minutes until the base is golden-brown.

Remove from the oven and leave to cool for a few minutes. Whilst still warm, use one of the chef's rings to stamp out 8 rounds of flapjack to use as bases, then leave them to cool completely. Leave the oven on.

For the filling, soak the raspberries in the whisky for 30 minutes.

In a large mixing bowl, whisk together the cream cheese and crème fraîche. Whisk in the honey, eggs and flour, then fold through the raspberries and any remaining soaking whisky. Spoon the mixture into the chef's rings on the baking sheet and bake in the preheated oven for 25–30 minutes until golden brown on top.

Leave to cool then transfer to the refrigerator to chill for at least 3 hours or preferably overnight.

When you are ready to serve, place a flapjack disc on each plate and top with a cheesecake. Serve with extra fresh raspberries, cream and a tot of whisky if desired.

COTTAGE CHEESE

Bright white in colour, with its characteristic, lumpy appearance and moist texture, cottage cheese – when made from skimmed/fat-free milk – has a reputation as the dieter's friend, valued for its low calorie count.

Making your own cottage cheese at home allows you to experiment with different milks. Using whole milk, for example, delivers a fuller-flavoured, creamier cottage cheese. Its soft texture means it can be spread easily, and it also lends itself to use in dips. A classic use of cottage cheese is simply as a clean-tasting filling for baked potatoes.

Innocuous in flavour, commercial cottage cheese is available both plain and in flavoured versions, with strong-tasting ingredients – such as ham, pineapple or chives – used to add a flavour punch. Plain cottage cheese makes an excellent base for improvising your own flavoured versions according to personal taste. Some of mine include: garlic and finely chopped herbs (parsley, chives and tarragon); chopped pitted olives and roasted red (bell) peppers; chopped cooked peeled prawns/shrimp, dill and lemon zest; flaked hot smoked salmon or mackerel. Enjoy these flavoured versions with crisp, crunchy rye breads for a Scandinavian-style snack. In many recipes, cottage cheese can be used instead of a béchamel to add a creamy texture – try it layered with pasta sheets and tasty ragù and baked to make lasagne – or seasoned well and mixed with other ingredients used as a filling in savoury pancakes.

Its fresh flavour also means that cottage cheese also lends itself to use in sweet dishes and desserts. An easy way to serve it is simply drizzled with a little runny honey or maple syrup and eaten with fresh fruit, such as chopped bananas, raspberries or strawberries or sliced peaches, either for breakfast or as dessert. Cottage cheese, whizzed with eggs, flour and sugar to make a smooth mixture, can also be used as the filling for a light-textured cheesecake. Cottage cheese can also be easily transformed into another indulgent treat by mixing it with eggs, milk and flour into a thick batter and frying spoonfuls of it dropped onto a hot greased frying pan/skillet to make small, soft-textured pancakes, excellent as a breakfast or brunch treat.

MAKING COTTAGE CHEESE

Cottage cheese retains some moisture after it's been made, which accounts for its characteristic texture. When making cottage cheese at home, you can experiment by using milks with different fat contents which will alter its flavour and richness.

ingredients

2 litres/2 quarts semi-skimmed/low-fat milk

5 drops liquid cheese-making rennet

2 tablespoons previously boiled and cooled water

2 tablespoons cultured buttermilk

salt, to taste

equipment

kitchen thermometer

large knife

ladle

muslin/cheesecloth

colander

makes about 350 g/1½ cups

Gently heat the milk in a large, heavy-based saucepan to 35°C (95°F), using the kitchen thermometer to check the temperature.

Mix the rennet into the cooled water and add it to the warm milk, stirring in thoroughly to disperse it well. Add in the buttermilk and stir in.

Cover with a lid and leave to stand for 1 hour at room temperature so that the mixture coagulates, forming a soft curd.

Using a large knife, cut the curd in the pan into roughly 2.5 cm/1 in. chunks.

Gently heat the curds to 43°C (110°F) and keep them at this temperature, stirring often, for 10 minutes.

Ladle the curds into a muslin-/cheesecloth-lined colander in the sink, and allow them to drain for 3–5 minutes.

Rinse the curds well under cold water, then fold up the muslin/cheesecloth around the curds and twist it to release excess water.

Transfer the curds into a shallow bowl and season with salt to taste, mixing in thoroughly. Cover and chill until required.

SPINACH & CHEESE BUREK

Burek is a baked or fried pastry, often surrounding a cheese and vegetable filling. Traditionally, in parts of Eastern Europe, burek is enjoyed with a glass of keffir, a type of drinking yogurt.

300 g/10 oz. fresh spinach (or 420 g/ 14 oz. frozen spinach, defrosted and drained)

110 g/½ cup cottage cheese

100 g/scant ½ cup Greek yogurt

1 large (UK)/extra large (US) egg, beaten

30 ml/2 tablespoons olive oil, plus extra to brush

30 ml/2 tablespoons sparkling water

½ teaspoon bicarbonate of soda/baking soda

1 teaspoon salt

250 g/8 oz. large filo/phyllo sheets

18-cm/7-in. square baking pan (4 cm/1³/4 in. deep), greased

makes 4-6 portions

Preheat the oven to 180°C (350°F) Gas 4.

Blanch the spinach in a saucepan of boiling water for 30 seconds. Drain and squeeze to get rid of excess water. Chop finely, then put in a mixing bowl with the cottage cheese, yogurt, egg, oil, water, bicarbonate of soda/baking soda and salt and mix well.

Lay a filo/phyllo sheet in the base of the baking pan, leaving the excess pastry hanging over one side of the pan. Brush with oil. Lay another sheet on top so that the overhang is on the opposite side of the pan. Spread a generous tablespoon of spinach mixture over the filo/phyllo sheet. Lay another 2 sheets over the filling and scrunch up the excess pastry to fit the pan. Brush with oil. Spread another generous tablespoon of spinach mixture over the filo/phyllo sheet. Lay another 2 sheets over the filling and scrunch up the excess pastry to fit the pan. Brush with oil. Keep going until all the spinach mixture is used up. You should end with a layer of filling.

Finally, fold over the overhanging pastry to cover the top of the burek and brush all over with more oil. If the top isn't entirely covered with pastry, add another sheet and brush with oil.

Bake in the preheated oven for 40 minutes until deep golden and risen. Remove from the oven and leave to cool for a few minutes. It freezes well – defrost and warm up in the oven before serving.

SERBIAN BUREK

This wonderful Serbian speciality is easy to make and always impresses dinner guests. Strong, barrel-aged feta cheese makes a fantastic filling if you can get it.

250 g/1 cup cottage cheese

60 g/2 oz. barrel-aged feta cheese, crumbled

190 g/¾ cup reduced-fat Greek yogurt

2 eggs, beaten

2 tablespoons olive oil, plus extra to brush

½ teaspoon bicarbonate of soda/baking soda

1½ teaspoons salt

6 large sheets of thick filo/phyllo (47 x 32 cm/18 x 12 in., see *Note*)

20-cm/8-in. springform pan (7 cm/3 in. deep), base-lined with parchment paper

makes 6 slices

Preheat the oven to 180°C (350°F) Gas 4.

Put the cottage cheese, feta, yogurt, eggs, oil, bicarbonate of soda/baking soda and salt in a mixing bowl and mix well.

Make sure there is plenty of space to work on. Take one filo/phyllo sheet and lay it on the work surface. Lightly brush it all over with oil. Place a second filo/phyllo sheet on top. Spoon one-third of the cheese mixture on to the filo/phyllo and spread it evenly across the surface, leaving the edges clear.

Fold over each short side by 2 cm/1 in.. Do the same with a long side, then carry on rolling it downwards (not too tightly) until you've rolled all the filo/phyllo and made a tube. Gently lift up the tube and curl around the inside edge of the cake tin. The filo/phyllo tears easily so try to lift it gently, but don't worry too much if it tears a little.

Repeat this entire process with the remaining filo/phyllo sheets, making 2 more tubes and fitting them end to end in the pan until you have a spiral. Brush the top with oil.

Bake in the preheated oven for 40 minutes until deep golden and risen. Don't worry if parts of the pastry look a little burnt, as this tastes really good. Remove the pan from the oven and let cool for a few minutes before serving.

Note The large sheets of filo/phyllo pastry can often be found in the freezer aisle of supermarkets. Let the pastry defrost for 1 hour before starting. If you can't find such large sheets, simply overlap your sheets to make the correct size and remember that you'll need more to begin with.

RICOTTA

An Italian cheese, ricotta has its roots in frugality, as it is made traditionally by using the whey left over after cheese-making. The name 'ricotta', in fact, means 're-cooked'.

Fresh ricotta is white in colour with a noticeably soft, pleasantly smooth texture and mild lactic flavour. It's also available in dry-textured salted and smoked versions. Although cow's milk ricotta is the one widely available, it can be made from the milk of sheep, goats and buffaloes. It is a very perishable cheese, so making your own ricotta allows you to enjoy it at its freshest.

In itself, ricotta has very little flavour, which makes it a very adaptable cheese – one that has many uses within Italian cuisine. Probably one the most common ways of encountering ricotta when eating out in an Italian restaurant is as a filling for fresh pasta – inside, say tortellini, cannelloni or ravioli, with ricotta's light texture making it a very elegant base for fillings. When used in this way, it is traditionally paired with cooked spinach and seasoned generously with aromatic, freshly grated nutmeg and umami-rich Parmesan cheese – a subtle and excellent combination. The use of ricotta as a filling in this way also crops up in a typical Tuscan dish: crespelle alla Fiorentina, where filled pancakes are coated in a tomato and béchamel sauce and baked. Ricotta, again partnered with spinach, is also traditionally used to make little dumplings, known as gnocchi, again characterized by their delicate flavour and texture.

When it comes to desserts, cakes and pastries, ricotta's lightness of texture and neutral flavour make it very versatile. The easiest way to serve it as a dessert is to sweeten it to taste, using sugar or honey, and serve it with fresh fruit, such as peaches or berries. Another simple use is to sweeten it and flavour it with freshly ground coffee, creating, in effect, a coffee 'mousse'. In Italy, ricotta is used to make assorted cheesecakes and sweet tarts, classically flavoured with ingredients such as vanilla, lemon zest or candied peel. On the sweet front, however, perhaps the best-known of ricotta's uses is in Sicilian cannoli. This is a much-loved pastry concoction in which crisp, deep-fried tubes of dough are filled with sweetened ricotta studded with pieces of dark chocolate and chopped candied peel – a glorious treat, enjoyed with a strong espresso coffee.

MAKING RICOTTA

Ricotta is a soft cheese from Italy, used in both savoury and sweet dishes, from filled pastas to Sicilian cannoli. Traditionally, it was made using the left-over whey from cheese-making, hence its name which means 'cooked again'. In the absence of whey, ricotta can be made very easily using whole milk.

ingredients

2.8 litres/3 quarts whole milk (cow's)

3 tablespoons white wine vinegar

½ teaspoon salt

equipment

kitchen thermometer

colander

wet muslin/cheesecloth

makes approx 450–500 g/ 1¾–2 cups

Place the milk in a large, heavy-based saucepan. Heat it slowly and steadily over a medium heat until it reaches 82°C (180°F) on your thermometer.

Remove the milk from the heat and stir in the vinegar and salt at once, mixing thoroughly.

The milk should begin to curdle. Cover and set it aside for 3 hours. Be sure not to move the pan during this time so that the curds will form.

Place a large colander in the sink and line it with a double layer of wet muslin/cheesecloth. Pour the curds into the colander and leave to drain in the sink for 2 hours, so that the excess moisture runs off.

Transfer the ricotta cheese into a bowl and use as required.

ricotta 97

RICOTTA & SPINACH DUMPLINGS
with cherry tomato sauce

Inspired by Italian cuisine, this recipe uses ricotta, together with spinach, to make little dumplings. The sauce here is a simple tomato one, flavoured with basil, lemon and a touch of chilli/chile for a hint of piquancy.

400 g/14 oz. fresh spinach

250 g/1 cup ricotta

2 eggs

100 g/³⁄₄ cup fine semolina, plus extra for coating

50 g/²⁄₃ cup grated Parmesan, plus extra for serving

salt and freshly ground black pepper

freshly grated nutmeg

butter, for greasing

for the cherry tomato sauce

2 tablespoons olive oil

2 garlic cloves, chopped

a splash of dry white wine (optional)

2 x 395-g/14-oz. cans of peeled cherry tomatoes

2 pinches of dried chilli/hot red pepper flakes or 1 peperoncino, crumbled

a generous handful of fresh basil leaves

a sprinkle of freshly grated lemon zest

serves 4

Rinse the spinach well, discarding any discoloured or wilted leaves. Place it in a large, heavy-based saucepan and cook, covered, over medium heat until the spinach has just wilted, so that it retains some texture. Strain in a colander, pressing out any excess moisture and set it aside to cool. Once cooled, chop the spinach finely, again squeezing out any excess moisture.

While the spinach is cooling, place the ricotta in a clean tea/dish towel in a sieve/strainer over a bowl to drain off any excess moisture.

For the cherry tomato sauce, heat the olive oil in a heavy-based frying pan. Add the garlic and fry, stirring, until golden brown. Add the white wine and cook, stirring, until it has largely evaporated. Add the cherry tomatoes, chilli/hot red pepper flakes and lemon zest. Roughly tear the basil (reserving a few leaves) and mix in. Season with salt and pepper. Cook, uncovered, for 5–10 minutes, stirring now and then until the sauce has thickened.

Place the ricotta in a large bowl and break it up with a fork. Mix in the finely chopped spinach thoroughly. Add the eggs, semolina and Parmesan and mix well. Season with salt, pepper and nutmeg and mix again.

Sprinkle semolina on a large plate. Take a teaspoon of the ricotta mixture and, using a second teaspoon, shape it into a little nugget. Still using teaspoons, place this ricotta dumpling on the semolina and roll, lightly coating it. Repeat the process until all the ricotta has been shaped into dumplings.

Preheat the oven to 190°C (350°F) Gas 5, and while it's preheating, gently reheat the cherry tomato sauce. Generously butter a heatproof serving dish and place it in the oven to warm through. Line a plate with paper towels.

Bring a large saucepan of salted water to the boil. Cook the dumplings in batches, adding them to the boiling water a few at a time – you shouldn't over-crowd the pan. Cook over medium heat until they float to the surface, around 2–3 minutes. Remove the dumplings using a shallow, slotted spoon, drain on the paper-lined plate, then carefully transfer to the serving dish in the oven to keep warm. Repeat the process until all the dumplings have been cooked.

Tear the remaining basil leaves and stir into the cherry tomato sauce. Serve the dumplings with the sauce and extra Parmesan on the side.

SWISS CHARD, RICOTTA & PINE NUT TART

Ricotta gives this delicately flavoured tart an appealing lightness. Serve it with little gem lettuce leaves and a creamy dressing topped with chopped chives.

50 g/$\frac{1}{2}$ cup pine nuts

300 g/10 oz. prepared shortcrust pastry/ pie dough

300 g/10 oz. Swiss chard

2 medium shallots

2 teaspoons olive oil

1 teaspoon balsamic vinegar

2 eggs, beaten

300 ml/1$\frac{1}{4}$ cups crème fraîche

50 g/$\frac{2}{3}$ cup grated Parmesan cheese

salt and freshly ground black pepper

freshly grated nutmeg

250 g/1 cup ricotta cheese, drained in a sieve/strainer to remove excess moisture

24-cm/9$\frac{1}{2}$-in. loose-based tart pan

baking beans

serves 6

Preheat the oven to 200°C (400°F) Gas 6.

Firstly, dry-fry the pine nuts in a small frying pan/skillet over a medium heat. Shake the pan every 20 seconds to avoid burning them. Remove them when they're golden on both sides, then set them aside.

Next, make the pastry case. Roll out the pastry/pie dough on a lightly floured work surface. Use the pastry/pie dough to line the tart pan. Press it in firmly and prick the base to stop it from bubbling up as it bakes. Line the case with a piece of baking parchment and fill it with baking beans. Blind bake the pastry case for 15 minutes. Carefully remove the baking beans and parchment and bake for a further 5 minutes.

While the pastry case is baking, prepare the filling. Rinse the Swiss chard, then place it in a heavy-based saucepan, cover and cook over medium heat, stirring now and then, until wilted. Drain it well using a colander, squeeze it dry and roughly chop.

Peel the shallots, halve lengthways and halve again crossways. Heat the olive oil in a separate small frying pan/skillet. Fry the shallots gently until softened, then mix in the balsamic vinegar and stir for 1–2 minutes until the shallots are glazed. Set aside to cool.

Lightly whisk together the beaten eggs, crème fraîche and Parmesan. Season with salt and pepper and add the nutmeg.

In the blind-baked pastry case, layer in the glazed shallots, then top with the Swiss chard. Dot the ricotta, in small pieces on top of the Swiss chard and sprinkle over the pine nuts. Pour in the egg mixture.

Bake for 40 minutes in the preheated oven until golden-brown and puffed up. Serve warm from the oven or at room temperature.

FIG & HONEY RICOTTA CHEESECAKE

Ricotta makes for a pleasantly light-textured cheesecake. Here it's combined with figs and honey to give a Mediterranean flavour. Serve it for dessert or enjoy it with coffee as a mid-morning treat.

150 g/5 oz. digestive biscuits or graham crackers

50 g/3½ tablespoons butter, melted

750 g/3 cups ricotta

2 eggs

2 tablespoons runny honey

½ teaspoon orange flower water

40 g/⅓ cup plain/all-purpose flour

6 fresh figs, halved

20-cm/8-in. loose-based cake pan

serves 6

Preheat the oven to 180°C (350°F) Gas 3.

Using a rolling pin, crush the biscuits into crumbs.

Use a large bowl to mix the crumbs with the melted butter. Next, press this mixture firmly and evenly into the cake pan to form a base.

In a separate large bowl, mix together the ricotta and eggs. Stir in the honey, orange flower water and flour.

Spoon the ricotta mixture evenly across the biscuit base. Now, press the halved figs, skin-side down, into the ricotta mixture.

Bake the cheesecake in the preheated oven for 50 minutes to 1 hour until set. Remove the pan from the oven and cool, then cover and chill until serving.

The cheesecake will keep for a few days, covered, in the refrigerator.

MASCARPONE

No wonder mascarpone has that indulgently smooth and rich texture and that lingering subtle, buttery sweetness – it's a cheese made from cream!

An Italian cheese, mascarpone is best-known for its use in a famous Italian dessert tiramisù, now found in restaurants around the world. The name means 'pick me up', a reference to the coffee contained in the dish. This indulgent creation is made by dipping Savoiardi biscuits (Italian sponge fingers, also known as ladyfingers) into strong espresso coffee flavoured with a shot of liqueur, such as Kahlua or brandy and layering them in a dish. On top of these one spreads a layer of mascarpone cheese which has been sweetened slightly, flavoured with vanilla and enriched with egg yolks and beaten until smooth. This layering is repeated, with the final layer dusted with cocoa powder and chilled until serving. The luxurious texture of the mascarpone, contrasted with the bitter coffee sponge layer, makes this a true treat. Nowadays, of course, there are numerous versions of tiramisù out there – flavoured with summer berries, chocolate (dark or white), limoncello – a testament to mascarpone's versatility

As one might expect, mascarpone's culinary use is that of an enriching element, adding both a luxurious texture and that subtle, rich complexity of cream that has been transformed into cheese. One simple but effective use is simply to stir a tablespoon of mascarpone into a freshly cooked risotto – such as an asparagus risotto or a courgette/zucchini and basil risotto – just before serving, so adding a creamy note. Similarly, it can be used in pasta sauces instead of double/heavy cream, where it works well with ingredients such as tomatoes, spinach and Italian cooked ham. Its smooth, spreadable texture means that it works well in dips – combined to good effect with ingredients such as piquant Gorgonzola and walnuts, with the mild sweetness of the mascarpone a subtly muting element.

Desserts, though, are where mascarpone comes into its own, used to make splendid cheesecakes, transformed into smooth-textured ice cream or flavoured with coffee, honey or liqueur and served with dainty biscuits and fruit. It also makes a luxurious accompaniment to desserts, served in place of cream, going well with dishes such as fruit pies, fruit tarts or cakes. For a taste of summer, serve dollops of mascarpone with syrup-baked figs or amaretto-stuffed peaches.

MAKING MASCARPONE

This soft, rich cheese is made from two types of cream. Although making mascarpone isn't complex it does require draining time, so factor this in when you're thinking of making and using it.

ingredients

450 ml/2 cups single/light cream

150 ml/⅔ cup double/heavy cream

2 drops liquid cheesemaking rennet

1 tablespoon previously boiled, cooled water

equipment

kitchen thermometer

muslin/cheesecloth

colander

makes about 320 g/1⅓ cups

Place the single/light and double/heavy creams in heavy-based saucepan.

Heat the mixture gently, stirring now and then, until it reaches 82°C (180°F) on the thermometer.

In a bowl, mix together the rennet and water. Add this diluted rennet to the hot cream and stir for 10 minutes, maintaining the temperature at 82°C (180°F).

Pour the hot cream mixture into a muslin/cheesecloth-lined colander in the sink, cover, and leave there to drain and cool for 1 hour.

Now place the colander with the cream mixture over a bowl or in a deep dish and set aside in the fridge for 6–7 hours or overnight.

Transfer the soft, thick, smooth-textured cheese in the colander into a dish, cover and chill until required.

SPAGHETTI WITH GORGONZOLA, PECAN & MASCARPONE SAUCE

The toasted pecan nuts add texture to this rich and creamy cheese sauce. Gorgonzola is a strongly flavoured blue cheese that is perfect combined with the milder mascarpone. Other blue cheeses you could use are Roquefort or even Stilton.

4.5 litres/4¾ quarts water

450 g/1 lb. dried spaghetti

25 g/2 tablespoons unsalted butter

1 garlic clove, peeled and crushed

175 g/6 oz. Gorgonzola, crumbled

175 g/¾ cup mascarpone

a pinch of ground mace or a little freshly grated nutmeg

salt and freshly ground black pepper

100 g/⅔ cup pecan nuts, toasted and roughly chopped

2 tablespoons chopped fresh chives

serves 4

In a large saucepan over a high heat, bring the water to the boil and add 2 teaspoons of salt. Add the dried spaghetti, allow the water to return to the boil before turning the heat down to medium. Cook the spaghetti for 10 minutes if you like it al dente and a couple of minutes longer if you like it softer.

Meanwhile, melt the butter in a saucepan and gently fry the garlic over low heat for 2–3 minutes, or until soft but not browned. Stir in the Gorgonzola, mascarpone, mace or nutmeg along with the salt and pepper. Cook gently until the sauce is heated through but the cheese still has a little texture.

Remove the pan from the heat and stir in the pecan nuts and chives. Season to taste, then add the cooked spaghetti and mix thoroughly. Serve immediately.

RHUBARB & MASCARPONE TART

Few things can compete with the first cut of outdoor-grown rhubarb every season – the pleasing sharpness of the fruit contrasts wonderfully well with the creamy mascarpone filling in this tart.

for the filling

500 g/1 lb. rhubarb, cut into 2-cm/1-in. slices

175 g/³/₄ cup caster/granulated sugar

30 g/2 tablespoons salted butter, softened

225 g/scant 1 cup mascarpone

30 g/¹/₄ cup plain/all-purpose flour

grated zest of 1 orange

2 eggs, separated

100 ml/scant ¹/₂ cup double/heavy cream

for the shortbread base

135 g/9 tablespoons salted butter, softened

65 g/¹/₃ cup caster/granulated sugar

160 g/1¹/₄ cups plain/all-purpose flour

15 g/2 tablespoons cornflour/cornstarch

25 g/3 tablespoons rice flour

for the syrup

2 teaspoons arrowroot

freshly squeezed juice of 1 orange

23-cm/9-in. loose-based tart pan

baking parchment

baking beans

serves 8–10

Preheat the oven to 190°C (375°F) Gas 5. Put the rhubarb for the filling in an ovenproof dish, sprinkle 60 g/¹/₃ cup of the sugar over the top and cover with foil. Roast in the preheated oven for about 15 minutes. Remove the rhubarb from the oven and strain it, reserving the juice for later. Set aside. Leave the oven on.

To make the shortbread base, put all the ingredients in a large bowl and rub together using your fingertips until it forms a paste. Knead gently into a smooth ball of dough (refrigerate it for a few minutes if it is too soft to work). Alternatively, put the ingredients in the bowl of a food processor or electric stand mixer and blend until it forms a smooth ball of dough. Roll out the pastry on a lightly floured work surface to form a circle about 5 cm/2 in. larger than the pan. Drape the pastry over the rolling pin and carefully transfer it to the tart pan. Gently mould the pastry into the base and sides. Trim the top edge with a sharp knife. Line the tart case with a sheet of baking parchment. Fill the tart case with baking beans and blind bake in the preheated oven for 15–20 minutes. Take out of the oven, remove the baking parchment and baking beans. When cool, line the sides of the tart pan with strips of baking parchment about 5 cm/2 in. high.

To make the filling, put the butter, remaining sugar, mascarpone, flour and orange zest into a large bowl. Beat until evenly mixed, then add the egg yolks and cream. Beat to a creamy consistency and set aside.

Put the egg whites in a grease-free bowl and, using an electric stand mixer or hand whisk, whisk the egg whites on high speed until light and foamy and soft peaks are formed. Transfer to the mascarpone mixture and whisk together, then spoon into the tart case. Distribute the rhubarb evenly over the filling. Bake for 40–45 minutes or until golden-brown and the filling is set like a hot soufflé – firm but with a slight wobble!

To make the syrup, stir together the arrowroot and 2 tablespoons water in a cup. Put the reserved rhubarb juice and the orange juice into a saucepan and bring to the boil. Remove from the heat and start stirring in the arrowroot – it may not all be needed, depending on how much juice you've produced from your rhubarb. The syrup should be just slightly thickened, as it thickens further with cooling.

Serve the tart warm with the syrup poured on top.

CARROT CAKE

Moist and wholesome with a pleasant sweetness, there's something honest and comforting about freshly-baked carrot cake.

150 g/³⁄₄ cup packed light brown soft sugar

1 egg

170 ml/³⁄₄ cup corn oil

140 g/1 cup plus 1¹⁄₂ tablespoons wholemeal/whole-wheat flour

¹⁄₂ teaspoon baking powder

1 teaspoon ground cinnamon

¹⁄₂ teaspoon freshly grated nutmeg

¹⁄₄ teaspoon salt

1 ripe banana, mashed

50 g/¹⁄₃ cup chopped walnuts

30 g/3 tablespoons sultanas/golden raisins

125 g/²⁄₃ cup grated carrots

for the topping

100 g/scant ¹⁄₂ cup mascarpone

40 g/¹⁄₃ cup icing/confectioners' sugar

10 g/2 teaspoons salted butter, softened

a squeeze of lemon or lime juice (optional)

grated lemon zest, to garnish

500-g/1-lb. loaf pan lined with a paper loaf-pan liner

serves 8

Preheat the oven to 170°C (325°F) Gas 3.

Put the sugar, egg and corn oil in a large bowl and lightly beat together. Add the flour, baking powder, cinnamon, nutmeg and salt and stir to a smooth mixture. Add the mashed banana, walnuts and sultanas/golden raisins, followed by the carrot, and stir together.

Spoon the mixture into the prepared loaf pan and bake in the preheated oven for 55 minutes. A skewer inserted into the middle of the cake should come out clean. Remove from the oven and allow to cool in the pan for about 15 minutes, then turn out onto a wire rack to cool completely.

To make the topping, put the mascarpone, icing/confectioners' sugar and butter into a bowl and whisk until light and creamy. If desired, add a squeeze of lemon or lime juice to bring a bit of zing to the frosting. Spread the topping over the cake and garnish with lemon zest.

This cake will keep for 5–7 days in the refrigerator.

FETA-STYLE CHEESE

Feta has been made in Greece for centuries; indeed it is so iconic a Greek cheese that in 2002 it was granted a Protected Designation of Origin (PDO). This ensures that feta can only be made in specific mountainous regions of Greece using sheep's or goat's milk from the herds that roam and graze there.

When made from sheep's or goat's milk, as is traditional, feta is notably bright white in colour. It is characterized by a specific texture – firm and yet also crumbly. It is also noticeably salty, due to the salting and brining process, which occurs as it is made and stored. To remove excess saltiness, simply soak it in cold water for around 10 minutes.

Within Greek cuisine, feta has many uses. One especially well-known, much-enjoyed dish featuring feta is a classic Greek salad or horiataki – where crumbled or sliced feta is combined with juicy tomatoes, slices of refreshing cucumber, olives, green (bell) pepper, chopped onion and dressed simply with olive oil and dried oregano. This makes for a simple but effective dish, evoking the sun-drenched world of the Mediterranean. Many Greek mezzes dishes feature feta in assorted forms, used as a filling in little tiropitakia (dainty, triangular, filo/phyllo pastry pies), and bringing a bite – in both texture and flavour terms, as it retains its texture when cooked – to fried courgette/zucchini fritters. Feta also brings its distinctive flavour to spanakotiropita, made by layering cooked spinach with crumbled feta, spring onions/scallions, dill and eggs between layers of filo/phyllo pastry. It is also the primary flavouring in a traditional cheese pie, circular in shape, made by coiling feta-filled pastry sheets. Prawns/shrimp saganaki partners feta with seafood, using it cubed and baked with prawns/shrimp in a tomato sauce.

Cheese in the feta style, often made from cow's milk, which gives it a milder flavour, is widely made around the world. When making it yourself, you can experiment with different milks, using sheep's or goat's or, indeed, a combination of sheep's, goat's and cow's milk. It's a gloriously versatile cheese to use in the kitchen – lending itself to simple salads, with its saltiness contrasting well with fruits such as watermelon, cantaloupe melons or nectarines or flavourful salad greens such as watercress or rocket/arugula. As one might expect, the Mediterranean palette of flavourings – olive oil, lemon, garlic, oregano and parsley – go very well with feta and it also has an affinity with Middle Eastern flavourings such as pomegranate molasses or za'atar. In addition to using feta straight away, one traditional way of preserving it and giving it a different depth of flavour is to store it in olive oil.

MAKING FETA-STYLE CHEESE

Making your own feta-style cheese at home requires time not only for the cheese to be formed, but also for it to acquire its characteristic salty flavour. The recipe opposite uses cow's milk, which gives a mild flavour. For tangier results, use goat's milk or sheep's milk.

ingredients

2 litres/2 quarts whole milk

2 tablespoons cultured buttermilk

10 drops of liquid cheesemaking rennet

2 tablespoons previously boiled water, cooled

6 tablespoons sea salt flakes

150 ml/^{2}/$_3$ cup olive oil (optional)

equipment

kitchen thermometer

large knife

slotted spoon

muslin/cheesecloth

colander

30-cm/12-in.

length of string

plastic container

sterilized glass jar

(optional)

makes about
300 g/3^1/$_3$ cups

Gently heat the milk in a large, heavy-based saucepan to 31°C (88°F). Add the buttermilk and stir it in thoroughly. Cover and set aside for 1 hour.

Mix the rennet with the cooled water, then add this to the milk mixture, stirring in well to disperse thoroughly. Cover and set aside in a warm place for 1 hour, which will allow the milk to turn into curd.

Using a large knife, cut the fragile curd in the saucepan into approximately 2.5 cm/1 in. cubes. Cover the pan and leave for 30 minutes in a warm place.

Using a slotted spoon, carefully transfer the soft curds to a muslin-/cheesecloth-lined colander in the sink. Wrap the muslin/cheesecloth up around the curd, forming a parcel. Now tie the parcel using string to a long wooden spoon laid across the top of a large, deep pot or bowl. Place the pot or bowl in the refrigerator to drain for 5 hours.

Unwrap the curd and cut into three even slices. Place the slices in a plastic container, sprinkle the curd generously with salt flakes, put the lid on the container and set aside at room temperature for 24 hours. During this time the salt will dissolve into a solution. Turn the slices over once during this period to ensure even salting.

Remove the cheese slices from the salt solution and rinse under cold water to wash off excess salt. Your feta is ready for eating. You can slice or cube it or add flavour by putting it in a sterilized glass jar and then covering the feta in olive oil.

BROAD BEAN, FETA & DILL SALAD

The season for fresh, young broad/fava beans is short. They need very little preparation; just throw them into some boiling water, rinse, drain and add to pastas, risottos and salads, among other dishes. Older and frozen broad/fava beans can be used but they need a little more attention as their skins are tougher.

500 g/1 lb. shelled fresh young broad/fava beans or butter beans

65 ml/¼ cup olive oil

1 small red onion, finely chopped

2 garlic cloves, finely chopped

2 tablespoons freshly squeezed lemon juice

a small bunch of fresh dill, finely chopped

a handful of fresh flat-leaf parsley leaves

a handful of small fresh mint leaves

100 g/1 cup roughly crumbled feta

freshly ground black pepper

serves 4

Cook the broad/fava beans in a large saucepan of boiling water for 10 minutes. Rinse under cold water and drain well. (If using older broad/fava beans, slip the skins off now and discard.)

Heat 1 tablespoon of the oil in a small frying pan/skillet set over a medium heat. Add the onion and garlic and cook for 2–3 minutes, until just softened. Remove from the heat.

Put the broad/fava beans and herbs in a bowl. In a small bowl, use a fork to mix together the remaining oil and lemon juice and then pour over the salad. Stir to combine. Add the feta, stir again, and season well with pepper before serving.

LEMON THYME &
FETA LOAF

This is a cross between a savoury bread and a cake. It rises
with baking powder a bit like soda bread, so it's really
simple to prepare. It's great on a hot day with gazpacho
or on a cold evening slathered with butter and served with
a warming spicy soup.

325 g/2½ cups plain/
all-purpose flour

2 tablespoons baking powder

1 teaspoon salt

200 ml/⅔ cup plus 2
tablespoons whole milk

150 ml/⅔ cup extra virgin
olive oil

2 eggs, beaten

1 large courgette/zucchini,
coarsely grated

125 g/1¼ cups crumbled feta

2 fresh lemon thyme sprigs,
leaves only

freshly ground black pepper

a 900-g/2-lbs. loaf pan,
lined with non-stick
parchment paper

makes a 900-g/2-lbs.
loaf

Preheat the oven to 180°C (350°F) Gas 4.

Sift the flour, baking powder and salt into a large bowl
and season with freshly ground black pepper.

In a measuring jug/pitcher, combine the milk and olive
oil and beat in the eggs. Stir into the dry ingredients
along with the courgette/zucchini, two-thirds of the
feta and half the thyme leaves. Stir until there are no
more floury pockets but don't overbeat it or you'll
make the mixture tough. Spoon into the prepared loaf
pan. Scatter over the remaining feta and remaining
thyme. Bake in the preheated oven for 1–1¼ hours, or
until a skewer inserted in the centre comes out clean.

Remove the pan from the oven and leave to cool for
10 minutes in the pan, then turn out onto a wire rack
to cool completely.

LAMB & ASPARAGUS TACOS
with roasted tomato salsa

Asparagus is not a traditional Mexican ingredient, but the shape of the spears makes an attractive filling. These are more elegant than the average taco and are perfect for entertaining.

700 g/1 lb. 9 oz. lean lamb, sliced (leg is best)

2–4 tablespoons vegetable oil

1–2 teaspoons ground cumin

500 g/1 lb. 2 oz. asparagus spears, tough ends removed

freshly squeezed juice of ½ lemon

8–10 corn tortillas, warmed

150 g/1½ cups crumbled feta

for the roasted tomato salsa

950 g/2 lbs. 2 oz. ripe tomatoes

1 large onion, thickly sliced

4 fresh green chillies/chiles

a small bunch of fresh coriander/cilantro

fine sea salt

a pinch of sugar

2 tablespoons freshly squeezed lime juice

ridged stove-top grill pan/griddle

serves 4

Put the lamb slices in a shallow dish and drizzle with 1–2 tablespoons of the oil. Sprinkle over the cumin and rub in evenly. Cover and leave to marinate in the refrigerator for at least 30 minutes, but preferably overnight. Return to room temperature before cooking.

To prepare the asparagus, heat the remaining oil over high heat in a large frying pan/skillet and add as many asparagus spears as will fit in a single layer – you may need to work in batches. Cook for 3–4 minutes on each side, without stirring, to char the asparagus. Transfer to a plate and repeat to cook the remaining asparagus. Before removing the last batch from the pan, squeeze over the lemon juice, cook for about 30 seconds then pour the pan juices over all of the cooked asparagus. Toss to coat evenly, season with salt and pepper to taste and set aside.

To make the roasted tomato salsa, first heat a ridged stovetop grill pan/griddle over a high heat. Add the tomatoes, onion and chillies/chiles and cook for 3–5 minutes on each side until charred all over. Put the onion, tomatoes, chillies/chiles, and coriander/cilantro in a blender and work to a coarse purée. Transfer to a bowl and stir in the salt, sugar and lime juice and set aside.

Preheat a ridged stovetop grill pan/griddle over high heat. When hot, add the lamb slices and cook for 2–3 minutes on each side to sear. Remove from the heat, season with salt and let stand for a few minutes.

To serve, place a few asparagus spears in the middle of each warmed tortilla, add a generous helping of sliced lamb and then sprinkle the crumbled feta over the top. Add a spoonful of the salsa and serve immediately with extra salsa on the side.

sources & suppliers

U.K. sources & suppliers

THE CHEESE MAKING SHOP
23 Prospect Lane
Solihull
B91 1HN
www.cheesemakingshop.co.uk
0121 744 4844

CRJ SOLUTIONS
A-1–8 Anglo Trading Estate
Commercial Road
Shepton Mallet
Somerset
BA4 5BY
www.cjsolutions.co.uk
01749 346 133

LAKELAND
Alexandra Buildings
Windermere
Cumbria
LA23 1BQ
www.lakeland.co.uk
015394 88100

MOORLANDS CHEESEMAKERS LTD
Lorien House
South Street
Castle Cary
Somerset
BA7 7ES
www.cheesemaking.co.uk
01963 350634

ORCHARD VALLEY DAIRY SUPPLIES
4 Lower Terne Business Park
Burford
Tenbury Wells
Worcestershire
WR15 8SZ
www.orchard-dairy.co.uk
01584 811137

U.K. raw milk supplier

PGT HOOK & SON
Longleys Farm
Harebeating Lane
Hailsham
East Sussex
BN27 1ER
01323 449494

U.S.A. & Canada sources & suppliers

GET CULTURE
501 Tasman Street, Madison, WI 53714
Telephone: 608-268-0462
Fax: 608-242-9036
www.getculture.com

THE CHEESEMAKER
11611 North Grace Court
Mequon, WI 53092
414-745-5483 (call/text)
www.thecheesemaker.com

GLENGARRY CHEESEMAKING & DAIRY SUPPLY
In Canada
P.O. Box 190, 5926 Hwy #34
Lancaster, Ontario, K0C 1N0

In the U.S.A.
c/o Margaret Morris, P.O. Box 92
Massena, NY, 13662
1-888-816-0903 or (613) 347-1141
Fax (613) 347-1167
www.glengarrycheesemaking.on.caa

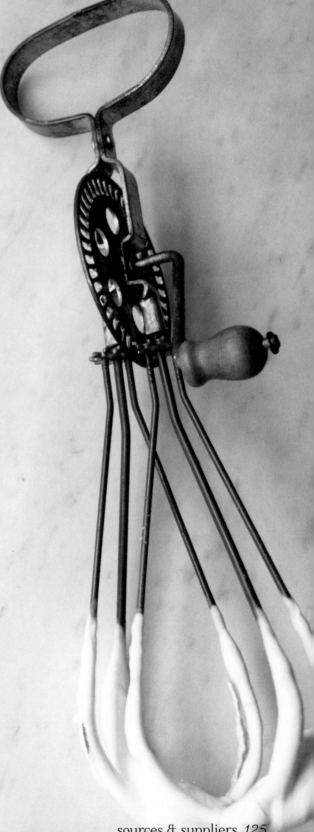

U.K. raw milk availability

Distribution of 'raw' (unpasteurized and unhomogenized milk) is legal in England, Wales and Northern Ireland, but illegal in Scotland. There are around 200 registered producers in England who sell raw milk directly to consumers, usually at a farm, a farmers' market or through a delivery service. Each bottle must legally display this warning: 'this product has not been heat-treated and may contain organisms harmful to health'.

U.S.A. raw milk availability

Federal law prohibits dairies from selling raw milk across state lines that has been packaged for sale to consumers.
This means that raw milk can only be distributed across state lines if it is going to be pasteurized or made into aged cheese. That said, each individual state makes its own laws about selling raw milk within its borders. A few states including California, Pennsylvania and Washington permit the sale of raw milk in retail stores. Many states, including Wisconsin, New York and Texas, allow farmers to sell raw milk directly to individuals. And some states, such as New Jersey and Iowa, forbid the sale of raw milk altogether. Check the website www.farmtoconsumer.org to learn about the status of raw milk sales in your own state. In Canada, raw milk is not permitted for sale to consumers.

(source: http://www.cdc.gov/foodsafety/rawmilk/raw-milk-questions-and-answers.html)

index

acknowledgments

Creating a book is always a team effort and my thanks go to Cindy Richards, Julia Charles and Nathan Joyce of RPS for commissioning me and for their editorial input. Many thanks, too, to photographer Clare Winfield, stylists Lisa Harrison and Rosie Reynolds and designer Iona Hoyle for transforming my text into such a lovely-looking book.